Helping Kids Achieve Their Best

T0373603

Helping Kids Achieve Their Best is a practical guide to motivating younger and older learners across the globe. The book explores why some students are easier to motivate than others and why students lose motivation, as well as outlining strategies that teachers can use in the classroom and that parents can use at home.

Comprehensively updated, this second edition includes a new chapter on student achievement emotion. Throughout the text, each chapter includes a variety of examples and research-based tools that can be put into action immediately, along with vignettes, question points, action stations, and recommended readings, which help educators apply the suggested approaches in their own contexts. The book is hands on and interactive, inviting readers to recall challenges they have faced in their own teaching or parenting experiences and to apply what they have learned to better understand and cope with these challenges more effectively.

This book is an essential resource for pre- and in-service teachers, as well as parents who aspire to motivate their children and help them achieve their best.

Dennis M. McInerney is an Honorary Professor at the Education University of Hong Kong. Prior to this, he was Chair Professor of Educational Psychology and Associate Vice President (Research and Development) and Co-Director of the Assessment Research Centre of the University. Professor McInerney continues research consultancies with a range of international universities and individuals.

Gregory Arief D. Liem is an Associate Professor at Psychology and Child & Human Development Academic Group, National Institute of Education, an institute of Nanyang Technological University. His research interest centers on understanding student motivation, engagement, and well-being through a sociocultural lens.

Helping Kids Achieve Their Best

Motivation – Theories and Practices

Second Edition

**Dennis M. McInerney
and Gregory Arief D. Liem**

Routledge
Taylor & Francis Group

LONDON AND NEW YORK

Cover image: Johan Alexander

Second edition published 2022
by Routledge
4 Park Square, Milton Park, Abingdon, Oxon, OX14 4RN

and by Routledge
605 Third Avenue, New York, NY 10158

Routledge is an imprint of the Taylor & Francis Group, an informa business

First edition published by Routledge 2000

British Library Cataloguing-in-Publication Data
A catalogue record for this book is available from the British Library

Library of Congress Cataloging-in-Publication Data
A catalog record has been requested for this book

ISBN: 9781032056173 (hbk)
ISBN: 9781032056166 (pbk)
ISBN: 9781003198383 (ebk)

DOI: 10.4324/9781003198383

Typeset in Bembo
by KnowledgeWorks Global Ltd.

To all the thousands of students who have taught me so much about motivation. Thanks!

(Dennis M. McInerney)

To my parents for laying the foundation of the 'right' form of motivation in me. I am always grateful.

(Gregory Arief D. Liem)

Contents

Foreword   x
Acknowledgment   xi

Introduction   1

1 What is Motivation?   2
Motivation and Its Impacts on Learning 3
Overview of Perspectives 4
Chapter Structure 6
Question Points 7
Action Stations 7
References and Recommended Readings 7

2 What's in It for Me?   9
Have You Encountered Similar Challenges? 10
What Might Be the Problem? 10
* Self-Determination Theory 11*
* Curiosity as a Need for Cognition 13*
* Personal Constructivism 14*
Things to Try 14
Question Points 19
Action Stations 19
References and Recommended Readings 20

3 Why Should I Do It?   21
Have You Encountered Similar Challenges? 22
What Might Be the Problem? 22
* Expectancy-Value Theory 23*
* High-Need and Low-Need Achievers 23*

*Negative Strategies Used to Avoid Failure by
    Low-Need Achievement Students 25*
*Negative Strategies Used to 'Guarantee Success' by
    Low-Need Achievement Students 25*
Things to Try 26
Question Points 28
Action Stations 28
References and Recommended Readings 29

4 Why Did I Fail?   **30**
Have You Encountered Similar Challenges? 31
What Might Be the Problem? 31
Things to Try 36
Question Points 38
Action Stations 38
References and Recommended Readings 39

5 I Believe I Can Do It   **41**
Have You Encountered Similar Challenges? 42
What Might Be the Problem? 42
Things to Try 43
    Modeling Self-Efficacy 45
    Peer Models and Self-Efficacy 46
    Self-Management and Self-Regulated Learning 47
Question Points 48
Action Stations 48
References and Recommended Readings 49

6 Stars, Stamps, and Jelly Beans   **50**
Have You Encountered Similar Challenges? 51
What Might Be the Problem? 51
Things to Try 53
    Potential Problems with Reinforcement 54
    Punishment and Learning 56
    Are There Appropriate Forms of Punishment? 57
    More Programmatic Approaches to Behavioral Teaching 58
    Direct Instruction as a Teaching Procedure 59
    Direct Instruction as a Cognitive Strategy 60
    Direct or Indirect Teaching? 60

Question Points 62
Action Stations 62
References and Recommended Readings 63

7 Shooting for Goals   **64**
Have You Encountered Similar Challenges? 65
What Might Be the Problem? 65
Things to Try 71
   Helping Students Set Goals 72
   Personal Investment in Achieving Goals 73
Question Points 74
Action Stations 75
References and Recommended Readings 75

8 How Do I Feel?   **77**
Have You Encountered Similar Challenges? 78
What Might Be the Problem? 78
   Anxiety and School Motivation 81
Things to Try 83
   Promoting Emotion Regulatory Skills 83
   Are There Effective Means of Alleviating Test Anxiety? 84
Question Points 87
Action Stations 88
References and Recommended Readings 88

9 But I Teach Well, Don't I?   **90**
Have You Encountered Similar Challenges? 91
What Might Be the Problem? 91
Things to Try 92
   Changing the School's and Classroom's Psychological
    Environment to Enhance Student Motivation 92
   Diagnosing Current School Practice 94
   Adolescence and School Motivation – Are There Special Issues? 95
Question Points 98
Action Stations 99
References and Recommended Readings 99

Index   101

Foreword

One of the most challenging tasks for prospective and seasoned teachers alike is motivating their students to learn. In this engaging and easy-to-read book, Dennis McInerney and Gregory Liem, internationally recognized experts on student motivation, provide readily accessible and common sense approaches to this task. Of the many books on motivation currently available, this one does an excellent job of engaging teachers to interact with the content in thoughtful and constructive ways. Each chapter begins with a realistic class-room vignette that describes a common motivational problem; after reviewing the relevant theory and research, the authors then ask readers to consider a series of questions that challenge them to think about how the problem arises in their own classrooms and ways in which they might address the problem most effectively. In doing so, they encourage classroom teachers to develop insights into why their students approach and engage in learning as they do, along with strategies for how to facilitate the development of more adaptive motivational styles.

In short, using current theory and research as foundational tools, the authors provide insightful ways to apply scholarship on motivation to the day-to-day practice of teaching. This is an excellent book for teachers who wish to understand the complex motivational issues that surround students' lives at school as well as to develop practical ways to help students approach learning tasks with a positive motivational outlook.

Kathryn Wentzel
University of Maryland

Acknowledgment

We thank Alexander Yohan for the creative illustrations we used in this book.

INTRODUCTION

Helping students achieve their best in our classrooms is not an easy task. It is a challenging process that requires us to consider multiple factors and forces before trying different strategies. This is because students come with a complex history which includes family, culture, health, physical, social, and emotional attributes, as well as prior learning experiences. These backgrounds orient them in new learning situations – sometimes positively and sometimes negatively. We cannot hope to fully understand the complexity of these factors and forces, but we can come to understand better some basic reasons that are likely to facilitate or impede a student's motivation and learning in the classroom. Our treatment of motivation, and our approach to putting together this book, is an attempt to help you to understand some of these more fundamental dynamics. The task is not easy as motivation in classrooms does not stand alone – it has deep roots that stretch back into the whole world of the child. Nevertheless, at times it is possible to define motivational problems in a classroom from a limited perspective and to implement strategies to help overcome the problems – strategies which do work! In this book, we outline various theories of school motivation, both contemporary and classic, and for ease of understanding we classify them into Cognitive, Social-Cognitive, Behavioral, and Humanistic perspectives. The theories of motivation that we cover in this book provide an armory of techniques, strategies, and skills to try with your students who appear to not want to learn. Used in concert, they are very powerful. Understanding factors and forces underlying motivation in the classrooms and using the corresponding strategies that promote it should improve the motivation and the quality of learning of your students. Let's begin our journey!

DOI: 10.4324/9781003198383-1

1 WHAT IS MOTIVATION?

John, a teacher educator was pondering over his lecture on motivation and wondering where to start, and if all the theories and practices covered in books were equally useful.

Jane, who shared workspace with him, said, 'All theories add to our understanding of what motivates children to learn. Best to cover them all.'

'Good point,' replied John, 'but where to start?'

Smiling, Jane responded, 'We can start by asking motivational issues that our student teachers encountered in their teaching experiences', and continued, 'We can then present the theories according to the issues they raise.'

John's face beamed and his eyes opened widely. 'Brilliant!', he enthusiastically exclaimed.

DOI: 10.4324/9781003198383-2

Everyone agrees that a key factor in successful learning is a learner's motivation. Everyone also agrees that a key factor in effective teaching is a teacher's ability to facilitate student motivation, particularly in circumstances where children are not inherently interested in learning (Fredricks, Reschly, & Christenson, 2019). However, there is limited agreement on what the essential elements of student motivation are, and what factors teachers should attend to in order to facilitate motivation in their students (Liem & McInerney, 2018, 2020).

A number of theoretical explanations of motivation have been developed over the past decades. They are of considerable assistance to teachers in understanding the nature of motivation and the dynamics of the motivational process in learning environments. These theoretical explanations are of great help in designing lessons and structuring learning experiences to optimize the motivation of learners. Other somewhat atheoretical explanations of motivation such as those based upon teacher craft and practical wisdom, as well as those based upon classroom research and observation that are not yet theorized – what we might call teacher's common knowledge – are also of great value. In this book, we consider a range of theories and their practical applications in learning environments.

MOTIVATION AND ITS IMPACTS ON LEARNING

All teachers are familiar with classes and individuals that are highly motivated. There is a zing and zeal in the air. No work seems too hard, too much, or too boring. Teachers and students work harmoniously and energetically. Attention is alert and focused. Highly motivated students persist at the task, desire high levels of performance, and come back to the task time and time again voluntarily.

We are also aware that there is great variation from individual to individual on level of motivation for particular tasks (indeed, this applies equally to students and teachers!). Some students just seem easier to motivate than others. Sometimes this variation appears to reflect students' confidence and readiness to learn, and sometimes it tells us something about their interests and values. Sometimes the variation appears to represent sex differences (e.g., girls appear more motivated in language activities and boys in construction activities), and sometimes it may be rooted in students' socioeconomic and family backgrounds.

We are also aware that a given individual varies in motivation from task to task. Often teachers excuse a student's poor performance academically by saying that he or she just is not motivated, only to see the child strive to be best at swimming or drama, or strive to be best for another teacher. Conversely, many students who are highly motivated academically show little motivation for sporting activities.

Lack of motivation for a particular task may be indicated through an individual's distractibility, disengagement, lack of involvement, resistance, sullenness, apparent laziness, completing work in a superficial way, and self-deprecation. Some children deliberately perform below their capacity and some others engage in self-sabotaging behaviors. The problem is not necessarily lack of motivation, but rather that students are motivated for the wrong reasons. Among the negative forms of motivation are motivation to avoid failure and protect one's ego, motivation to increase stimulation through other activities than the one that should be the focus of attention, motivation to resist and not to participate, and even motivation to cause distractions to others!

Relative to their more motivated peers, poorly motivated students often have poorer views of their academic abilities (i.e., negative academic self-concepts), stronger insecurity about their ability to fit in at school or other learning environments, and higher subjective perceptions that school is not for them. Unfortunately, as students move through schooling, many appear to lose the motivation they had in earlier grades. What is it that schools and teachers do, or do not do, that seems to demotivate so many of their students? Why is it that some children maintain motivation even in difficult circumstances, while others give up easily?

Obviously, if we knew with certainty what motivated individuals in particular situations and could package this information, we would make a fortune. Alas, no one has, or will ever, come up with the magical formula.

We again must ask 'what is motivation?' Research and theory have yielded insights helpful to us in our quest to understand motivation, unpack its elements, and use them to promote deep engagement and effective learning.

OVERVIEW OF PERSPECTIVES

The word 'motivation' originates from the Latin word *movere* which simply means 'to move.' Many early perspectives on motivation were concerned with the functions of instincts, needs, and drives in influencing individual behavior. In this early research, researchers implanted electrodes in animal brains to stimulate their sex, hunger, and thirst drives, or balloons in animal and human stomachs to examine hunger drives. These researchers sought to 'motivate' their subjects through physiological means. While these early basic experiments have not led to educational environments, in which student motivation is enhanced through electrical stimulation, they did provoke us to think about some important motivational issues. For example, what 'energy' actually initiates motivated action? Is this 'energy' psychological, physiological, or a combination of both? What channels the direction of motivated behavior so that it becomes focused? What sustains motivated behavior once it has begun? Why does motivated behavior weaken or stop at particular times? And is motivation a necessary element of every learning activity?

These questions enable us to think about motivation in various contexts. While there is general agreement that motivation represents psychological and/or physiological forces that energize and direct behavior towards a certain goal, psychologists have developed major theoretical perspectives on human psychology including motivated behavior. These primary perspectives, which underpin more specific theories of motivation covered in this book, include *Cognitive Theory, Social-Cognitive Theory,* and *Behavioral Theory.* Each of these major perspectives has produced a number of interpretations of the genesis and maintenance of motivation, as well as key elements in its understanding. Suffusing each of these is a fourth perspective, *Humanistic Theory.*

Cognitive theories emphasize mental processes and perceptions as important elements of motivation and the personal construction of the meaning of experiences, which impacts an individual's motivation. Implied in cognitive views of motivation are a concern with a learner's need to make sense of ideas as well as develop and understand them as coherent and comprehensible knowledge.

Social-cognitive theories, while emphasizing individual mental processes, perceptions, and beliefs as sources of motivation, also highlight the role of sociocultural contexts in facilitating these processes and shaping individual perceptions and beliefs. These contexts include the social and emotional support of significant others such as parents, teachers, and peers, as well as the societal and cultural expectations and goals that these significant others model and that students learn, internalize, and make as their own. The impact of role models and anticipated consequences on motivated behavior are also regarded as important sources of motivation in social-cognitive perspectives of motivation.

Behavioral theories emphasize the external environment of the individual and how it motivates behavior through systems of reward and punishment. These perspectives highlight the non-cognitive aspect of the individual. In short, individuals are motivated because of the effect that rewarded or punished behavior has on them. Behavior that is rewarded becomes motivated behavior for individuals as they seek to repeat their previous pleasant experience (i.e., to obtain the reward again). Conversely, behavior that is followed by punishment becomes motivated behavior that individuals seek to not perform again in similar circumstances (i.e., to avoid future punishment).

Humanistic theories primarily focus on the importance of the individual's inherent desire for self-growth, which motivates behavior, and the importance of significant others and social environments in fostering the process of this self-growth. Humanistic approaches to understanding motivation, however, incorporate features of cognitive, social-cognitive, and behavioral perspectives in so far as they emphasize that individuals have the desire to make sense of their life experiences; that individuals introspect about the causes of their successes and failures; that individuals' perceptions of life experiences and their emotions orient their motivation; and that the effort to satisfy basic needs motivates behavior.

In the following chapters, we will present more specific theories of motivation representing these major perspectives. These specific theories include Self-Determination Theory (Chapter 2), Expectancy-Value Theory (Chapter 3), Causal Attribution Theory (Chapter 4), Self-Efficacy and Self-Regulated Learning Theories (Chapter 5), Behavioral Theories (Chapter 6), Achievement Goal Theory (Chapter 7), and Achievement Emotion Theory (Chapter 8), among others. None of these theories, on its own, is sufficient to explain the complexity of student motivation. In combination, however, they provide a great deal of insights into the nature of motivation in learning contexts and how it might be elicited, maintained, and promoted. Further, while these theories provide a broad or general framework to understand what drives students to learn, student motivation takes place in a socio-cultural and educational context. Applications of these theories, therefore, have to take into consideration their contexts and have to be understood through a contextual lens. We encourage you to consider the context of your teaching while applying theories, principles, and strategies discussed in this book.

Some overlap in key ideas and concepts of specific motivation theories have to be acknowledged. Indeed, this is reflected in this book in that many of the points made interlock with principles and strategies covered in several chapters. Our goal, however, is to make the theories as accessible as possible by clearly demonstrating their applied value for interpreting motivational problems, and for developing adaptive teaching techniques to alleviate these problems. We also hope to make the text interactive, and you will benefit most if you take the time to actively complete each of the activities presented.

CHAPTER STRUCTURE

Each of the following chapters has seven sections. We start with a brief *Vignette* that describes a motivational problem in the classroom, and some text which sets the scene for key motivational issues focused on in the chapter. Following this vignette, we then ask you to recall, *Have You Encountered Similar Challenges?* We then introduce you to key ideas of motivation theories in *What Might Be The Problem?* from which you will gain theoretical insights about the motivational problems discussed. *Things to Try* follows – this section provides you with potential strategies to solve the motivational problems encountered earlier and they are derived from theoretical lenses. Each chapter then presents a series of *Question Points* to challenge your interpretations or to encourage you to reflect on applications, and *Action Stations* to gain further insights into the issues covered in the chapter. Finally, we provide a list of *References and Recommended Readings* in order for you to develop your ideas and deepen your understanding further.

We hope the book helps you understand some of the important elements of what motivates students and their relationship to effective learning. We hope it serves as an insightful reference in promoting your students' motivation to learn in the classroom, and beyond.

QUESTION POINTS

?	What do you see in your role as a teacher in motivating students? Is it part of your professional responsibility and moral obligation to motivate your students to learn?
?	Consider the best class you ever had. What were the things that made this a good place for you to teach and for your students to learn?
?	Some teachers rationalize: 'Why should I break my neck to teach children who just do not want to learn?' How might the impasse be resolved? Do some teachers operate under misconceptions of their role?

ACTION STATIONS

* Before we commence our discussion of aspects of motivation, use the following table to list down the key strategies that you use to motivate individual students. Are some strategies more effective than others?

Student	*Strategies*	*Reasons*	*Outcomes*

* Consider some 'hard-to-motivate' students in your classroom. What are their characteristics? What strategies have you tried to motivate them? Have they worked? Why or why not?

  List your strengths and weaknesses as a teacher. How would these impact your students' motivation and the effectiveness of their learning?

REFERENCES AND RECOMMENDED READINGS

Anderman, E. M. (2021). *Sparking student motivation: The power of teachers in rekindling a love of learning.* Thousand Oaks, CA: Corwin.

Baumeister, R. F. (2016). Toward a general theory of motivation: Problems, challenges, opportunities, and the big picture. *Motivation and Emotion, 40,* 1–10.

Meece, J. L., & Eccles, J. S. (Eds.). (2010). *Handbook of research on schools, schooling, and human development.* New York, NY: Routledge.

Elliot, A. J., Dweck, C. S., & Yeager, D. S. (Eds.). (2017). *Handbook of motivation and competence: Theory and application* (2nd ed.). New York, NY: Guilford Press.

Ertmer, P. A., & Newby, T. J. (2013). Behaviorism, cognitivism, constructivism: Comparing critical features from an instructional design perspective. *Performance Improvement Quarterly, 26,* 43–71.

Ford, M. E., & Smith, P. R. (2020). *Motivating self and others: Thriving with social purpose, life meaning, and the pursuit of core personal goals.* Cambridge: Cambridge University Press.

Fredricks, J. A., Reschly, A. L., & Christenson, S. L. (Eds.). (2019). *Handbook of student engagement interventions: Working with disengaged students.* London: Academic Press.

Lazowski, R. A., & Hulleman, C. S. (2016). Motivation interventions in education: A meta-analytic review. *Review of Educational Research, 86,* 602–640.

Liem, G. A. D., & McInerney, D. M. (Eds.). (2018). *Big theories revisited 2.* Charlotte, NC: Information Age Publishing.

Liem, G. A. D., & McInerney, D. M. (Eds.). (2020). *Promoting motivation in contexts: Sociocultural perspectives on motivation and learning.* Charlotte, NC: Information Age Publishing.

Renninger, K. A., & Hidi, S. E. (Eds.). (2019). *The Cambridge handbook of motivation and learning.* Cambridge: Cambridge University Press.

Schunk, D. H., Meece, J. R., & Pintrich, P. R. (2014). *Motivation in education: Theory, research, and application* (4th ed.). Upper Saddle River, NJ: Pearson.

Wentzel, K. R. (2020). *Motivating students to learn* (5th ed.). New York, NY: Routledge.

Wentzel, K. R., & Miele, D. B. (2016). *Handbook of motivation at school* (2nd ed.). New York, NY: Routledge.

Wentzel, K. R., & Ramani, G. B. (Eds.). (2016). *Handbook of social influences in school contexts: Social-emotional, motivation, and cognitive outcomes.* New York, NY: Routledge.

Wong, Z., & Liem, G. A. D. (2021). Student engagement: Current state of the construct, conceptual refinement, and future research directions. *Educational Psychology Review.* Advance Online Publication.

2 WHAT'S IN IT FOR ME?

'I'm bored! This is so boring!', muttered Martin to his mate as he listlessly penciled in the answers to an exercise.

Nearby, Annette wasn't even pretending to complete the exercise, but rather was distracting anyone close enough to be flicked by little pieces of paper she had meticulously rolled into balls moistened with her saliva.

Mr. Thomas, the teacher, was aware that not all students were properly involved in the exercise, but he was used to this. His philosophy was 'if you had some of the students attentive some of the time you were doing well.'

The lesson ground to a slow and tedious finish and the students let out a 'whoop' as they rushed out to the playground to play.

Teachers and others debate the relative importance of internal and external motivators to student motivation. People do appear to have a natural

DOI: 10.4324/9781003198383-3

tendency to be self-motivated when learning material that is personally relevant and meaningful, and when they perceive that they have some personal control over their learning.

Individuals' motivation is broadly classified into *intrinsic* or *extrinsic motivation*. Generally referred to as that motive that keeps individuals at a task in and of itself because of their interest in the task, intrinsic motivation is a complex concept with many interpretations of what constitutes it and what its underlying processes are. With intrinsic motivation, the process of learning becomes substantially self-sustaining. Extrinsic motivation, on the other hand, represents a drive to attain outcomes beyond the interest in the task itself. It is a "means to another end" form of motivation. From an extrinsic motivation perspective, a key to an individual's motivation may lie in students' desire to get good grades and they see this as instrumental to achieve another goal such as receiving praise, outperforming peers, pleasing parents, or entering the university.

HAVE YOU ENCOUNTERED SIMILAR CHALLENGES?

In your own words, recall and describe your classroom teaching experiences in which your students were not motivated and engaged.

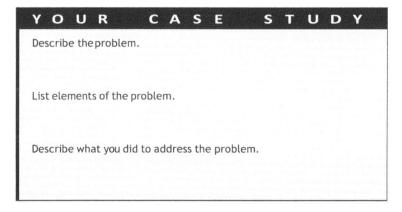

YOUR CASE STUDY

Describe the problem.

List elements of the problem.

Describe what you did to address the problem.

WHAT MIGHT BE THE PROBLEM?

What if the process of learning is not self-initiated and self-sustaining and students show little interest? At times, we teach students who appear uninterested in a particular learning activity. At other times, we have students who appear to have little interest in anything being taught to them. They do not become involved in the task and do not value the activity. Personal goals for achievement are set very low, if at all, and there is little attempt to improve in the activity.

Many of these situations in which students lack motivation are transient and of no importance, and motivation improves over time with a change in

circumstances, teachers, activities, and so on. At times, however, lack of interest and intrinsic motivation for learning is persistent and is related to more
deep-seated personal characteristics of the learner, which require considerable attention from the teacher in order for them to be alleviated. A key reason
why some learners do not become personally engaged in their learning is that
they fear failure and feel anxious. These negative thoughts and feelings are
exacerbated in classrooms characterized by competition, public evaluation,
and poorly thought out lesson plans and work exercises that do not take into
consideration students' interests or level of competence. Negative feelings
may also be contributed to by a number of social factors including the peer
group and family, and we will discuss some of these influences later in the
book. Many students let negative thoughts (e.g., doubting their capacity to
achieve or doubting the usefulness of the activity) to dominate their thinking
so that at times learning becomes a threatening chore to do and interest in
learning tasks becomes minimal. These negative 'mindsets' may be specific
to particular subjects or learning situations or generalized to many.

In our next section, we discuss Self-Determination Theory, which provides deep insights into intrinsic motivation and how important it is to student success at learning. The theory gives many insights into what we can do
to help understand and alleviate motivational blocks in children so that they
immerse themselves in learning.

Self-Determination Theory

The Self-Determination Theory is a contemporary motivation theory proposed by Richard Ryan and Edward Deci (2017, 2020). Self-Determination
Theory proposes that individuals have a fundamental, innate desire to grow
and thrive. The theory assumes that individuals have inner motivational
resources in the forms of interests, preferences, values, and goals and that
they are born with three basic psychological needs that, when satisfied, facilitate their readiness to learn and to flourish. These three psychological needs
are the *need for competence* (i.e., the desire to feel that one is capable and able
to master a task well), the *need for autonomy* (i.e., the desire to feel that one
has the freedom to choose what to do and decide on how things should be
done), and the *need for relatedness* (i.e., the desire to feel that one has genuine and warm connections with others). The degree to which the learning
environment satisfies students' needs for competence, autonomy, and relatedness, the more intrinsically motivated the students become. Intrinsically
motivated students engage in a task because of the enjoyment, satisfaction,
and pleasure they feel while doing the activity. They find the task fun and
interesting! As a result, they engage in high-quality learning and are persistent when facing challenges. They are enthusiastic and willing to spend long
hours on a task.

Extrinsically motivated students, on the other hand, are driven to study
for various reasons. These reasons, according to Self-Determination Theory,

are related to the positive or negative consequences that students expect to receive or avoid by doing an activity. Extrinsically motivated students try to complete a task because of the reward that they anticipate receiving or the punishment that they try to avoid (see also Chapter 6 – *Stars, Stamps, and Jelly Beans*). This reward or punishment may come from their teacher or parents in various forms (e.g., a longer recess time as a reward for the completed classwork or a shorter one as a punishment for the uncompleted classwork). Other extrinsically motivated students are driven to study because they do not want to feel guilty or ashamed for neglecting their work or, in contrast, because they want to feel 'good' about themselves for accomplishing it (e.g., feeling proud or relieved). And yet, other extrinsically motivated students put in the effort because they want to get a good grade! As much as it is pleasing to the teacher who teaches these grade-oriented students, they may become unmotivated when their effort does not pay off, especially when the grading system is norm-based.

Self-Determination Theory also points to the possibility that some students are *amotivated*. These students do not have a clear reason or goal for studying. They 'go through the motions' in their learning, simply because they are expected to do so, without having a genuine interest and enthusiasm. Understandably, amotivated students engage in low-quality learning and do not persist in the face of challenges.

As explained earlier, Self-Determination Theory assumes that students have inner motivational resources in the forms of needs, interests, preferences, values, goals, which, when satisfied, expressed, or pursued, promote the students' readiness to learn. Reeve and Cheon (2021) believe that it is through using an *autonomy-supportive* motivating style that facilitates the satisfaction or expression of these internal motivational resources that teachers can foster their students' intrinsic motivation.

Autonomy-supportive teachers are teachers who try to put themselves in their students' shoes by facilitating the congruence between students' inner motivational resources and their day-to-day classroom activities and, at the same time, still provide structure in the form of plans, rules, guidance, directions, as well as standards and expectations. Autonomy-supportive motivating style subsumes the following principles:

- *Nurturance of motivational resources.* Autonomy-supportive teachers nurture students' inner motivational resources by 'putting themselves in their students' shoes' in order to know and understand the students' interests, preferences, and levels of competence, and by creating a learning environment and designing classroom activities that are aligned with their students' characteristics.
- *Language use.* Autonomy-supportive teachers use informational and non-controlling language that is competence-affirming and information-rich to explain why students are doing well and how they can make progress.

- *Communication of values and rationale of tasks.* Autonomy-supportive teachers make an explicit effort to identify and explain the use and importance of a lesson for daily experiences (e.g., for health, relationship, community, and personal growth).
- *Acknowledgment of, and response to, students' negative affect.* Autonomy supportive teachers acknowledge and accept negative affect (e.g., anxiety and frustration) as a valid response to a challenging schooling process, and harness the situation to provide guidance and clarify steps needed for improvement and success.

Curiosity as a Need for Cognition

One of the important attributes of intrinsically motivated students is their curiosity. The hierarchy of human needs proposed by Abraham Maslow (1968) is a model of motivation that is known to many. However, few are aware of the presence of cognitive needs in his expanded model (Maslow, 1971). According to the hierarchy of needs, individuals are motivated by their desires to satisfy their unmet *biological and physiological needs* (e.g., the desire for air, food, drink, shelter, and sleep), *safety needs* (e.g., the desire for personal, family, and environmental security and stability), *belongingness and love needs* (e.g., the desire for warm and genuine interactions with others), *esteem needs* (e.g., the desire for respect and appreciation from one's self and others), *cognitive needs* (e.g., the quest for knowledge, understanding, and meaning), *aesthetic needs* (e.g., the desire for beauty, balance, order, and symmetry), *self-actualization needs* (i.e., the desire to realize one's potential and pursue a task that is aligned with one's interests, values, goals, and strengths), and *transcendence needs* (e.g., the desire to help others to grow).

The first four needs (i.e., biological, safety, belongingness, and esteem needs) are classified as *deficiency needs* that represent the needs that motivate people to get into action when they are unmet. The next four needs (i.e., cognitive, aesthetic, self-actualization, and transcendence needs) are classified as *growth needs* that represent the needs with an unlimited capacity for satisfaction and motivate people to seek further fulfilment. The implication of this motivation model is clear: the biological, safety, belongingness, and esteem needs of our students must be adequately satisfied before they are ready to learn and pursue their cognitive needs.

As a special case of the cognitive needs, curiosity plays an important motivational role in student learning. Curiosity has been defined as an individuals' awareness of the presence of a knowledge gap that serves as a motivator to find and acquire the information to fill the identified gap. In the school setting, curiosity represents students' desire for missing information to resolve the unknown, that is, to close the discrepancy between the students' current knowledge and what they wish to know (Murayama, FitzGibbon, & Sakaki, 2019; Shin & Kim, 2019). Curious students may feel excited and are likely to engage in exploratory and information-seeking behaviors in response to an information gap, with the purpose of reestablishing their cognitive equilibrium. However, the information gap in curious students might lead them to the state of cognitive disequilibrium and emotional discomfort (e.g., feeling uncertain, anxious, confused, or even frustrated) when the students do not receive appropriate support and scaffolding from the teacher. It is thus important for teachers to trigger the level of students' curiosity that is within an 'optimal zone' and to provide them with the necessary support and scaffolding so as to ensure that the students' motivation to satisfy their curiosity is sustained, or even fostered, over time.

Personal Constructivism

The notion of curiosity is well aligned with how learning occurs, or knowledge develops, according to personal constructivism that was first elaborated by Jean Piaget (1977). Although personal constructivism is predominantly known as a learning theory, it can also be applied to understand student motivation. This perspective emphasizes the active role of the learner in building or constructing knowledge and understanding or making sense of the world. Knowledge is not something that teachers can directly transmit to learners, but something that learners must mentally process, manipulate, and transform in order to have meaning for them. So, children are assumed to be intrinsically motivated to learn and construct their knowledge in response to their life experiences. They do not need rewards, or any other forms of intervention, from or by adults to be motivated. The role of the teacher is to help guide the knowledge construction process by focusing attention, posing questions, and stretching the learner's thinking by way of asking the learner to analyze, compare, or apply.

As a perspective on motivation, personal constructivism highlights the arousal of cognitive disequilibrium as a means to motivate students to learn something new and develop their knowledge. When a student faces a problem, for example, they experience a state of cognitive disequilibrium which brings about a desire to solve it, because the disequilibrium creates a sense of discomfort in the student. Teachers, therefore, need to create an optimal state of cognitive disequilibrium by posing questions that will make students recognize the gap in their thinking that they are motivated to close. Thus, it is important that teachers tap and build on the students' prior knowledge to help the students construct new knowledge.

THINGS TO TRY

Let us start with simple situations and simple solutions to the apparent lack of interest some learners show in their learning activities. If we consider that the source of the lack of interest in the learning task is boredom or perceived lack of relevance, there are a number of strategies to try. First, you can stimulate student involvement in learning by using variety in your teaching methods (e.g., group work, peer tutoring, games, and simulations), by allowing students some choice and control over their learning related to method, pace, and content, and by setting the task that is optimally challenging. This would meet the students' needs for relatedness, autonomy, and competence. In particular, it is very important to situate learning in relevant 'real life' contexts and to build on students' prior knowledge and interests such that students develop a sense of ownership in their learning. Active involvement by students in learning activities is also very important to stimulate interest, and you can engineer active involvement through the development of appropriate learning activities.

Another means of increasing student interest in learning activities is to stimulate curiosity in classroom activities. Curiosity is a major element of intrinsic motivation. Curiosity is stimulated by situations that are surprising, incongruous, or out of keeping with a student's existing beliefs and ideas. I (Dennis) was once enthralled by a teacher motivating a class to write a creative composition. He had a large black box of furry, feathery, squishy, squashy, hard, long, and thick objects. Each child had to put his or her hand through a small hole, feel an object, and then go back and write a short story on what had been felt. The pupils were spellbound and could not wait to have their turn and write their story. On another occasion, the same teacher had a large treasure chest in which there was an assortment of items. He drew one out at a time while telling a pirate story. Each of the items was part of the story. Interest was very high as students were asked to predict what would come out of the box next.

Another technique is to utilize fantasy, make believe, and simulation games in your learning activities. The success of the ABC program *Play School* illustrates this (see https://www.abc.net.au/abckids/shows/play-school/). Young children spend a lot of time reciting nursery rhymes and singing songs heard on *Play School*, their only reward being the joy of singing new songs and doing new things. Often classrooms are set up as shops to teach about money, or students prepare a class newspaper to learn about journalism. Many of the computer software programs now available capitalize on fantasy and simulation in order to captivate the interest, attention, and motivation of the user. Curiosity, fantasy, and simulations elicit what has been termed *situational interest* in the task, which facilitates motivation. Children's play is a clear opportunity to observe intrinsic motivation at its best. In fact, if the parent or teacher structures the play by telling children what to do or what resources to use, it may no longer be intrinsically motivating, and therefore, no longer 'play.'

It is important to note that the use of highly motivating techniques should not be at the expense of the substance of learning. In other words, a lot of razzmatazz may be highly interesting and motivating, but unless it is used to support meaningful learning activities then the use of such techniques is educationally valueless. Furthermore, techniques used to enhance the presentation of a learning activity should not be so distracting as to conflict with the purpose of learning. For example, when a teacher sets up a competition to stimulate interest, some students become more concerned with the competition and scoring points for their work, than with the quality of work they are completing. Often students enjoy participating in an educational game without trying to derive any academic benefit from it. Many multimedia computer software programs and mobile game applications are very entertaining but provide little in the way of 'educational content.' It is important, therefore, that situational interest generated by such techniques be converted to the topic or task interest, which will be relatively enduring for the students.

Other classroom practices that have been associated with developing students' intrinsic motivation include, for example, giving students the opportunity to be actively involved in the lesson through manipulation of objects; cooperative group work and presentations; providing immediate feedback to students on their work so that they see how well they are going; allowing students enough time to finish work properly and achieve goals; and providing students with the opportunity to interact with peers in a variety of learning situations such as role-plays, dramas, debates, and simulations.

You should model an *interest in learning* and a *motivation to learn* by being enthusiastic, interested in the tasks being presented, and curious. You should also show interest (and dare we say excitement!) at what students initiate. Indicate to students that you expect them both to enjoy their learning and to be successful. Students' natural motivation to learn will also be enhanced if you provide a safe, trusting, and supportive environment. This would be characterized by quality relationships in the classroom, learning and instructional supports that are tailored to individual needs, and opportunities for students to take risks without fear of failure.

As we have discussed earlier, students may have negative 'mindsets' about learning and who they are as learners. Perhaps the students can't see the connection between the activity and their daily lives. Perhaps the students feel the activity is too hard, or that they lack ability (or they *think* they lack ability!), or perhaps they are afraid of evaluation and failure. Negative thoughts such as these are very detrimental to motivation and many students get trapped into a syndrome in which feelings of confidence, interest, and excitement in learning are negated. In these circumstances, students need to take control of their negative thought processes so that they begin to value themselves as learners. Learners can be taught to understand and control their thinking so that they can step outside these negative beliefs about their abilities and fear of failure and become motivated. In other words, students can be taught which thoughts to pay attention to and which to discount. This has been termed *metacognitive awareness*. We deal with metacognitive awareness in greater detail later in the book.

There are, therefore, two basic elements in helping students replace negative thoughts with neutral ones (i.e., when they at least give themselves the benefit of the doubt) and then with positive ones (i.e., when they actually begin to think well of themselves as learners). The first element involves personal thought changing through active teacher–student dialogue. Through this process, there is an attempt by the teacher to guide students to value themselves, to grow to understand their thinking and motivational processes, and to see themselves as active agents in their own learning. Through this process, students become less insecure, which 'frees up' their natural motivation to learn (recall that, according to Maslow's hierarchy of needs, students must feel safe before they are ready to learn!). In particular, the teacher and student discuss specific problem areas that might affect motivation – 'the teacher doesn't like me,' 'the subject is too difficult,' 'I lack ability' – and how these thoughts may or may not reflect realities. In these discussions that you have with your students, you would consider the individual students' unique needs, interests, and goals and, specifically, have the students clarify these for themselves.

Although it is important for you to empathize and put yourself in your students' shoes, try to remain somewhat detached from what the student says. In other words, do not take students' negative reactions to particular events and circumstances personally, as sometimes these will involve you. In this way, you will have the opportunity to address and resolve misconceptions and help the student address issues over which he or she has control. Furthermore, it will give you information to help you restructure learning experiences so that some level of success is guaranteed for the individual in order for negative experiences, which often underlie negative thoughts, to become positive.

This brings us to the second and very important element related to the above. It involves restructuring learning activities so that students with negative thoughts begin to experience success and joy in learning and make the connection between effort and achievement. Older views of motivation assumed that teachers could motivate behavior through external controls, rewards, and performance comparisons. These approaches are often counter-productive for students with negative thoughts about their capacity to learn, since one of the major reasons for these is their supposed lack of ability and success, and lack of reward when their performance is compared to others. There is evidence that teachers who are more autonomy-supportive and less controlling, and who provide opportunities for student autonomy, initiative, and self-expression, create more effective environments for learning and motivation. This approach is most appropriate for students with negative thoughts. In the following sections, we outline some of the ways in which you can restructure learning activities so that opportunities for autonomy, initiative, and self-expression provide the student with positive learning experiences that facilitate the re-emergence of intrinsic motivation.

For individuals who lack confidence to be motivated in a particular task, the task must involve a level of challenge that is suited to their perceived capacity so that their skills are put to an appropriate test. This level needs to increase in challenge as the individual becomes more proficient. You should therefore help the learner to set challenging but realistic goals.

It is a truism that we work best at things we are interested in, relatively good at, and have control over. It is important, therefore, for a student to have a choice in and control of activities. The busy, productive work of students engaged on projects in groups is a measure of their intrinsic interest. It is also essential that you provide students with meaningful feedback about their performance in terms of their ability and effort on the task. It can also be very useful to provide opportunities for students with negative thoughts about their capacities to interact with peers and to share their thoughts and feelings. Most importantly, you need to provide opportunities for these students to develop autonomy in their learning by providing a safe, trusting, and supportive environment and communicating an expectation of success to students.

It is essential that you reduce social comparison by avoiding external and public evaluation and by emphasizing achievement in terms of personal best rather than comparative norms reflected through grades and marks. For this purpose, you need to use a range of measurement, evaluation, and reporting schemes. Using evaluation that relates to personalized improvement and the 'real world' of the student will also help the student develop a sense of self-efficacy in his or her learning. We look at this issue more closely in Chapter 5 (*I Believe I Can Do It*).

It is very important that you establish what are realistic expectations on 'reasonable effort' and help students establish realistic goals. Emphasize personal effort as the means for improvement and help students see that mistakes are part of learning. You can also promote beliefs in competence by helping students develop metacognitive and self-regulatory skills. It is very important to communicate positive expectations and make plans with students for self-improvement or personal progress.

Finally, you will increase students' chances for success if you model learning approaches and motivation in the classroom. It is useful to teach learning skills and strategies. Individualizing instruction and using cooperative and peer learning situations have also been found to be very useful in helping students experience success and to see the link between effort and achievement.

As we have indicated above, it is important to let learners experience a sense of agency in their learning. Therefore, it is essential that students are called on to take responsibility for and develop a sense of ownership of their learning within a learning environment which supports such student initiatives. You should encourage students, therefore, to reinvent a learning experience, and if necessary, to create interest and challenge in it when they find it boring or irrelevant. Encourage students to look for ways to make a task interesting. Tell them not to wait to be told what to do, but to take the initiative to make it interesting, fun, and worthwhile for themselves. Encourage them to be curious, to ask questions about what they are doing, and to ask for feedback on learning progress. Encourage them not to put up with feeling uncertain – they should express their concerns, clarify, and get help when they need.

When becoming involved in a task, students should expect success and work towards this. They should be assisted in sharing ideas and tasks with others and in setting both short-term and long-term goals that are realistic. Importantly, they should be given plenty of time to finish what they start.

QUESTION POINTS

?	Do you know what the interests of the students in your class are? How might you find out what their interests are? How would you use this knowledge in planning your teaching/learning activities?
?	Can you recall when you found your students deeply curious? What did you do at that time? How does that experience help you prepare and facilitate their curiosity in your next lesson?
?	Do you think your students feel respected, valued, and appreciated in the classroom? What can you do to make your students feel safe to be more ready to learn?

ACTION STATIONS

- Of central importance to motivation is interest in the learning exercise. Interest may be generated in a number of ways. For example, relating new material to a student's needs and existing capabilities often fosters interest. Moderate levels of challenge, relating learning experiences to the 'real world,' and the perceived importance and relevance of the learning to the individual also facilitate interest. Observe and discuss with a classroom teacher the ways in which interest is gained and maintained in the classroom. Record your observations.

- Observe a range of television programs specifically aimed at children (e.g., 'Sesame Street,' 'The Simpsons,' 'Playschool'). Also, observe a range of commercials directed at the same age groups. List the elements of motivation you see demonstrated in these programs. What principles of motivation seem to be used most often in these programs to engage, maintain, and increase the children's interest and attention? Do these vary according to the age group targeted? Illustrate how these same principles may be used effectively in the classroom.

- Find out about your students' personal needs, interests, and goals that influence their motivation and learning. Among the ways you could do this are individual interviews, class discussions, and interest surveys. You could, for example, ask your students:

  - What they do for fun.
  - What they feel about themselves (e.g., *I am happiest when I …; the best thing about me is …; the worst thing about me is …; I get angry when …; I feel important when …; I don't like to …*).
  - The skills and abilities they perceive they are strong and weak in.
  - What they value.

- Select an academic task and translate it into a particular student's interest and language. Try on a task that appears to be potentially perceived as boring and irrelevant to the student.

Task	Interest	Language

- Evaluate your curriculum from the point of view of a student. How interesting is it? How relevant and valuable does it appear? Would all students expect to be successful at the curriculum tasks? How could you change your curriculum to make it more interesting, relevant, valued, and achievable?
- Revisit your personal case study and describe your new insights and solutions.

REFERENCES AND RECOMMENDED READINGS

Kaufman, S. B. (2020). *Transcend: The new science of self-actualization.* New York, NY: The Guilford Press.

Maslow, A. H. (1968). *Toward a psychology of being.* New York, NY: D. Van Nostrand Company.

Maslow, A. H. (1971). *The farther reaches of human nature.* New York, NY: The Viking Press.

Murayama, K., FitzGibbon, L., & Sakaki, M. (2019). Process account of curiosity and interest: A reward-learning perspective. *Educational Psychology Review, 31,* 875–895.

Piaget, J. (1977). *The development of thought: Equilibration of cognitive structures. (Trans a. Rosin).* New York, NY: The Viking Press.

Reeve, J., & Cheon, S. H. (2021). Autonomy-supportive teaching: Its malleability, benefits, and potential to improve educational practice. *Educational Psychologist, 56,* 54–77.

Reeve, J., Ryan, R. M., & Deci, E. L. (2018). Sociocultural influences on student motivation as viewed through the lens of self-determination theory. In G. A. D. Liem, & D. M. McInerney (Eds.). *Big theories revisited 2* (pp. 31–60). Charlotte, NC: Information Age Publishing.

Renninger, K. A., & Hidi, S. E. (Eds.). (2019). *The Cambridge handbook of motivation and learning.* Cambridge: Cambridge University Press.

Ryan, R. M., & Deci, E. L. (2017). *Self-determination theory: Basic psychological needs in motivation, development, and wellness.* New York, NY: Guilford Publishing.

Ryan, R. M., & Deci, E. L. (2019). Brick by brick: The origins, development, and future of self-determination theory. In A. J. Elliot (Vol. Ed.), *Advances in motivation science* (Vol. 6, pp. 111–156). Cambridge, MA: Elsevier Inc.

Ryan, R. M., & Deci, E. L. (2020). Intrinsic and extrinsic motivation from a self-determination theory perspective: Definitions, theory, practices, and future directions. *Contemporary Educational Psychology, 61,* 101860.

Shin, D. D., & Kim, S.-I. (2019). Homo curious: Curious or interested? *Educational Psychology Review, 31,* 853–874.

3   WHY SHOULD I DO IT?

Martha was discussing her assigned work with Tony and intimated that she really could not care less about doing the literature assignment. 'You know, Tony, learning about Keats and Shelley is really pretty stupid and Mr. Briggs is a dumb teacher! I'm not going to ever read their poems, and, anyhow, at Uni I am going to do science.'

Tony, meanwhile, was only half concentrating on what Martha was saying as he mused to himself 'I wonder if I can con mum into taking me to the library after school to get some special resources on Keats and Shelley? The Internet might have some good material – gee I wish Martha would stop yacking so I can get off and do some work on my literature assignment.'

You have probably pondered at times on why two students of similar ability approach a learning task quite differently. One is highly motivated,

DOI: 10.4324/9781003198383-4

enthusiastic to set goals for achievement, and willing to take risks. The other appears to deliberately perform below their ability, choosing simple tasks, avoiding risks, and, in general, not engaging with the activity.

HAVE YOU ENCOUNTERED SIMILAR CHALLENGES?

Have you experienced a similar situation in your classroom? Describe a similar problem from your own classroom experience below.

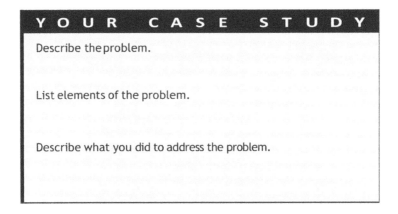

YOUR   CASE   STUDY

Describe the problem.

List elements of the problem.

Describe what you did to address the problem.

WHAT MIGHT BE THE PROBLEM?

How much a learner expects and values success in learning activities will influence his or her motivation and achievement. John Atkinson's (1964) early work on Expectancy-Value Theory provided some very valuable insights into the motivational process in school settings, especially in relation to the interaction of personality and environment in determining motivated behavior. Atkinson's goal was to predict whether an individual would *approach* or *avoid* an achievement task. He proposed that each individual has a tendency to achieve success and a tendency to avoid failure. This tendency is moderated by the individual's expectancy of success or failure on a particular task and by the incentive value of the task. The disposition an individual has in seeking success or avoiding failure is considered to be relatively stable. However, the actual dynamics of this mix depends on the two variables, namely, the individual's expectation of success or failure on the task and the value of the task to the individual. Both of these are subject to environmental variation and can be influenced by the teacher.

In short, the Expectancy-Value Theory tries to explain what it is that causes some individuals to perform certain behaviors and others not to, when both are equally able to do so. Not only is the expectation of success important, the value of that success in terms of anticipated rewards or punishments is also something that the individuals consider before committing to a task. For example, we probably all know of someone who has tried to give up smoking. The motivation to persist at this difficult task over a period of time is very much influenced by how successful they think they will be, and how personally valuable that success will be in terms of its rewards including, for example, having pleasant breath, greater social acceptability, and less risk of serious health problems, or its negative consequences such as experiencing unpleasant withdrawal side effects, increased hunger and potential weight gain, and a sense of bowing to social pressure?

Expectancy–Value Theory

Since its original conception, the Expectancy-Value Theory has been developed further and applied to educational settings by Jacquelynne Eccles and Allan Wigfield (Eccles & Wigfield, 2020; Tonks, Wigfield, & Eccles, 2018; Wigfield & Eccles, 2020). They have explored three components of the value of a task (or a subject): *attainment value*, representing the importance of doing well on the task to the person; *intrinsic value*, representing the inherent, immediate enjoyment one derives from the task; and *utility value*, representing the perceived relevance of the task and doing well on it to a future goal such as advancing one's career prospects. Research by Eccles, Wigfield, and their colleagues has shown that the value of a task is positively related to achievement-related choices. For example, girls who value Science, Technology, Engineering, and Mathematics or STEM-related subjects are more likely to take advanced courses in these areas than those with lower appreciation of these areas. However, when expectancy of success and value of the activity are used to predict success, it is a person's expectancy beliefs that are more significant predictors. It appears, therefore, that while values may be important in the initial choice of activity (one does not usually get involved in activities that have little value or interest), the expectancy of success appears to be more important than values as a factor in motivation after that (see Chapter 5 – *I Believe I Can Do It*).

High–Need and Low–Need Achievers

Atkinson (1964) proposed two theoretical personality types: the person for whom the need to achieve is greater than the fear of failure, and the person for whom the fear of failure is greater than the need to achieve. The first is labelled *high-need achiever* and the second *low-need achiever*. For high-need achievers, situations of intermediate challenge are most motivating. However, for low-need achievers, tasks of intermediate challenge appear most threatening and they often choose tasks that are far too hard so that the resulting failure can be excused, or tasks that are so easy that success is guaranteed.

In his Self-Worth Theory, which is based on Atkinson's model of motivation, Covington (1992, 1998; Covington, von Hoene, & Voge, 2017) believes that students' achievement behaviors are driven by a motivation to maintain the feeling of competence and self-worth. That is, students have the general tendency for maintaining their sense of positive self-worth by choosing a task that is attainable and/or avoiding anything that implies incompetence such that they would always feel competent. The ways in which students respond to a perceived threat of failure on an academic task determine the motivation styles they adopt. Covington calls high-need achievers *mastery-oriented* or *task-focused* students, whereas low-need achievers are *self-worth-focused* or *failure-avoiding* students. These two broad groups of students differ in the factors to which they attribute or explain their successes or failures (see Chapter 4 – *Why Did I Fail?*).

To better understand the difference between high-need and low-need achieving students, let us take a look at the following two children. A child from an achievement-oriented minority ethnic group may have a strong disposition to achieve success, which is related to cultural expectations, parental encouragement, peer models, and so on. In this context, school learning will have a very high value for this student as a means of achieving academically (and ultimately, economically). In a school setting that encourages his or her efforts, the expectation of success will therefore be positive and translated into motivated behavior. In contrast, a student from another minority group who expects not to have a job in the mainstream society because of perceived or anticipated prejudice may be less likely to value school learning and may expect little success in a school which holds low expectations of these students.

Furthermore, our schools and homes can be anti-intellectual places where *tall intellectual poppies* (or even short ones) can be cut down very quickly. Some students fear the peer ridicule which school success may bring them. In some cases, this ridicule may also come from family members. In this instance, academic success, which we as teachers consider a desirable outcome of learning, becomes something to be avoided.

When children begin school, most of them expect to be successful and value school learning enormously. As a consequence, motivational levels are usually very high and subsequent motivated behavior, reflected through effort and persistence, can be quite intense. What is essential for the teacher at this time is the selection of materials and exercises that guarantee success so that the child's personal expectations for success in relevant and meaningful activities are reinforced. However, there will be some students for whom early experiences have been unsuccessful so that there is a reduced expectation of success. These students may develop to become *learned helpless* or *failure-accepting* students (Covington, 1992, 1998; Covington et al., 2017). Learned helpless students attribute their performance on a task to their perceived lack of abilities (see Chapter 4 – *Why Did I Fail?*). Nevertheless, if these students value academic skills, knowledge, and achievement strongly and want to be successful, they can still be highly motivated. In these cases, carefully designed and monitored learning activities are essential to guarantee these students success so that the expectation of future success – and hence motivation – is enhanced.

However, for some students a reduced expectation of success and a heightened fear of failure, coupled with a lowered valuing of learning at school, can lead to a situation where the student's desire to avoid failure is stronger than their need to achieve. This can lead the student into a range of strategies inimical to learning successfully. We will discuss these detrimental strategies below.

Negative Strategies Used to Avoid Failure by Low-Need Achievement Students

Some low-need achieving students refuse to participate or waste time (e.g., sharpening pencils, erasing, looking for books, decorating the page, and so on so that time for learning runs out). Some refuse to answer questions rather than risking wrong answers. Others may engage in apparent effort so that they will get praise for busy work and at least avoid substantial reproof for failure. Some students set irrationally high goals (e.g., selecting activities that are too hard) in the belief that no one can be blamed if they fail because the task is obviously too difficult. Others hold a 'couldn't care less' attitude to avoid personal criticism or any real test of his or her ability.

In this last case, the teacher may reprimand lack of effort, thereby implying that, with effort, the student could do better in the future. This reprimand, in a sense, helps the student feel good because it suggests, in a public way, that the teacher believes that the student has ability. In other words, by not trying, students create an alternative explanation for failure, leaving open the question of whether they could have done better if they had tried. These students protect their self-worth by not trying. As a result, they do not know the true boundaries of their competencies because they never test them.

As you can see from this discussion, many students spend an enormous amount of their motivational energy avoiding failure rather than directing it into positive learning activities. In other words, these students engage in *self-handicapping* or *self-sabotaging* strategies such that, when failing on a task, they can protect their ego by attributing their performance on 'legitimate' causes other than their own ability.

Negative Strategies Used to 'Guarantee Success' by Low-Need Achievement Students

Some students 'guarantee success' by setting low goals, such as choosing material which is so simple that success is assured. In other words, these students 'play safe' by choosing an easy task on which success is guaranteed. Yet, other students over-strive through the use of extravagant effort to enhance the likelihood for success. Other students cheat. In this case, students give the impression that they are working diligently on worksheets when, in fact, they might be getting the answers by asking other students or by copying neighbors' answers. In this way, students manage to complete the assignment without any real understanding. Academic cheating is a particularly severe problem as the student needs to continue to cheat in the future to ensure 'success,' meanwhile falling further behind. Teachers can be fooled for quite a while.

Such negative coping strategies are used to preserve a sense of self-worth in competitive situations and are commonly used by failure-avoiding students in our classrooms. All of these coping strategies are antithetical to positive motivation and effective learning. No doubt you have seen these, at one time or another, in effect in your classrooms. Instead of allowing these negative strategies to flourish, we should show students the value of learning and ways of dealing with difficulty and temporary failure. I (Dennis) remember one individual who was an able but not brilliant student preparing for the final high school exams. Over the months leading up to the exams he was becoming more and more seriously fatigued. On talking to him, I discovered that he was getting about three hours' sleep per night. The rest of the time was spent in study to ensure he would not fail in the levels he had chosen to do for the examinations. With considerate advising and parental consultation, the student reshaped his expectations and work schedules so that he could cope with the task of preparing for the tests in a healthier fashion. This meant a reassessment of the need for success and the fear of failure for that student – not an easy personal readjustment in a competitive academic climate such as final exams.

THINGS TO TRY

One of our responsibilities as teachers is to assist students to set realistic and challenging goals and to ensure that students experience success at least a lot of the time. In terms of Expectancy-Value Theory, this will reinforce the student's perception that success can follow from effort, even if tasks may appear difficult. Of course, there need to be appropriate incentives for the student to make an effort: these should be negotiated with the student and may be designed as individual contracts.

It is worth keeping in mind that students with a low expectancy of academic success often defy classroom and school rules since the value of academic achievement is low relative to, for example, the value of status among their peers. For such students, threats of detention, suspension, or even expulsion from school are not disincentives: it is more motivating to have the (negative) attention from the teachers and schoolmates than to try to achieve academically and fail publicly.

What is integral to this negative motivation is a student's fear of failure and the need to protect his or her sense of self-worth. To help prevent the use of the self-defeating strategies described above, it is essential for you to remove the threat of failure and its potential negative impact on the learner's sense of self-esteem. You need to have the learner experience success. In addition, learning activities designed and presented to the student should be ones that enhance the value of learning. From the Expectancy-Value Theory, among some of the strategies that would be useful are the following:

Expectancy: 'If I try hard, what are my chances of success?'

Teachers should help students identify the behaviors or learning strategies that are associated with successful learning, for example, asking questions, searching for answers from knowledgeable sources, reflecting on learning progress, and checking for understanding. Do not let individual students do exercises that are too easy or too difficult. Guide students to activities with optimal levels of challenge for their individual ability while encouraging them to take risks without fear of failure. We define *optimally challenging tasks* as tasks that can be successfully accomplished by students with manageable effort and necessary scaffolding or support. You should provide opportunities for students to gain experience in decision making, risk and benefit analysis, and progress monitoring. You should also model risk-taking behavior and appropriate methods for handling mistakes and failure. Guide them to see that failure is part of learning. Try to challenge students to move forward into different and more difficult types of activities while avoiding 'put downs' when they take risks or propose ambitious projects. It is also important to try to eliminate 'put downs' by other students. You should teach strategies for learning and metacognition and bolster expectation of success as a result of personal actions. Give exercises that allow the students the opportunity to see their skills improving and to experience feelings of success, mastery, and competency. This process will be enhanced if you scaffold learning by providing appropriate support. Finally, you should avoid competitive situations by setting individualized tasks and personalized learning goals so that social comparison among students becomes more difficult.

Values: 'To what extent will I get something I want, or avoid something I don't like if I do this? If I work hard and reach the desired standard, do I really care?'

Teachers should clarify with the student the relationship between actions and consequences, and provide appropriate rewards and recognition for effort, improvement, and achievement in a number of areas. These rewards should be provided equitably across the class. It is useful to encourage students to select their own rewards. Counsel students as to the long-term consequences of effort, self-improvement, and academic achievement, and support students in long-term success goals in situations where parental support may be lacking.

Teachers should assist students to diagnose the values they place on academic achievement and relate this to the effort they expend. Students become more motivated when they are aware of the meaning and importance of the task assigned to them. In other words, make sure that students see the links between what they are doing in school and what they wish to do and achieve in the future. Students will be more motivated when they are able to see the relevance of schooling and what they learn in school to their daily lives and future. Reinforce student's awareness of negative consequences for not making efforts in learning, and help them value and accept success that can be attributed to their own ability, effort, and effective strategies. It is important that students see the positive consequences of their effort for achievement.

QUESTION POINTS

> **?** Which do you believe is more important for your students' motivation on a task: expecting success or valuing success?

> **?** Consider how expectancy beliefs and subjective task values under different effort conditions (low, medium, and high) may explain differential motivational levels in your classroom.

ACTION STATIONS

- Reflect on your own motivation and performance levels in particular activities. How adequate is the Expectancy-Value model as an explanation of your personal motivation and performance?
- It appears from research that one key to successful learning and motivation is a student's understanding of the learning process. In other words, successful motivated learners are able to step back from their learning and monitor what they are doing. They appear to be strategic and can call upon a number of cognitive and behavioral strategies to assist with their learning. As it is clear that metacognitive skills are learned, greater attention is being paid by teachers today to the teaching of learning skills and monitoring of learning process. In this activity, we want you to discuss with other teachers how they teach students to learn. Make a list of these techniques. Then interview two students while they are working on a problem (which could be in mathematics, science or language) and ask them to describe how they are going about solving the problem. Make verbatim notes and try your hand at interpreting each student's use of metacognitive skills (assuming they are using any).
- Repeat the exercise with students whom you observe as well-motivated and success-oriented, students whom you categorize as poorly motivated and failure-avoiding, and students whom you see as disengaged and failure-accepting. Are there any patterns characterizing the use of learning strategies in these different groups of students?
- Revisit your personal case study and describe your new insights and solutions after reading this chapter.

REFERENCES AND RECOMMENDED READINGS

Atkinson, J. W. (1964). *An introduction to motivation.* Princeton, NJ: Van Nostrand.

Covington, M. V. (1992). *Making the grade. A self-worth perspective on motivation and school reform.* New York, NY: Cambridge University Press.

Covington, M. V. (1998). *The will to learn: A guide for motivating young people.* New York, NY: Cambridge University Press.

Covington, M. V., von Hoene, L. M., & Voge, D. J. (2017). *Life beyond grades: Designing college courses to promote intrinsic motivation.* New York, NY: Cambridge University Press.

Eccles, J. S. (2009). Who am I and what am I going to do with my life? Personal and collective identities as motivators of action. *Educational Psychologist, 44,* 78–89.

Eccles, J. S., & Wigfield, A. (2020). From expectancy-value theory to situated expectancy-value theory: A developmental, social cognitive, and sociocultural perspective on motivation. *Contemporary Educational Psychology, 61,* 101859.

Tonks, S. M., Wigfield, A., & Eccles, J. S. (2018). Expectancy-value theory in cross-cultural perspective: What have we learned in the last 15 years. In G. A. D. Liem, & D. M. McInerney (Eds.). *Big theories revisited 2* (pp. 91–115). Charlotte, NC: Information Age Publishing.

Wigfield, A., & Eccles, J. S. (2020). 35 years of research on students' subjective task values and motivation: A look back and a look forward. In A. J. Elliot (Ed.), *Advances in motivation science* (Vol. 7, pp. 162–193). New York, NY: Elsevier.

Wigfield, A., Eccles, J. S., & Möller, J. (2020). How dimensional comparisons help to understand linkages between expectancies, values, performance, and choice? *Educational Psychology Review, 32,* 657–680.

Wigfield, A., & Gladstone, J. (2019). How students' expectancies and values relate to their achievement in times of global change and uncertainty. In E. N. Gonida & M. Lemos (Eds.), *Motivation in education at a time of global change: Theory, research, and implications for practice. Advances in motivation and achievement* (Vol. 20, pp. 15–32). London: Emerald.

Wigfield, A., Rosenzweig, E., & Eccles, J. S. (2017). Achievement values. In A. J. Elliot, C. S. Dweck, & D. S. Yeager (Eds.), *Handbook of competence and motivation: Theory and application* (2nd ed.) (pp. 116–134). New York, NY: Guilford Press.

Wigfield, A., Tonks, S. M., & Klauda, S. L. (2016). Expectancy-value theory. In K. R. Wentzel, & D. B. Miele (Eds.), *Handbook of motivation at school* (2nd ed.) (pp. 55–74). New York, NY: Routledge.

4   WHY DID I FAIL?

'I didn't study for the test' was a common claim among the students fronting-up to Mrs. Bridge's physics test. In some cases, the claim was true, while in many others it was quite false. But in any event, it was a good ploy to avoid embarrassment if, in fact, one didn't do well. It nicely allowed one to sidestep the implication that one was not bright enough to do physics. If, happily, one did extremely well then the 'fact' that 'one hadn't studied' made the achievement all the better – 'You must be oh so bright!'

Some students believe that they lack ability in particular activities and no amount of effort or practice will help them to become successful. Failure

DOI: 10.4324/9781003198383-5

is often attributed to perceived lack of ability. Such attitudes are obviously negative and debilitating. It is an irony that when these same people are successful, they often attribute their success to good luck or to the easiness of the activity. But, on the whole, they avoid involvement in activities in which their perceived lack of ability is likely to be a major cause of their performance. As you will see, there are different 'causes' that students may use to explain their performance on a particular academic task, and these 'causes', determine their subsequent motivation and learning.

HAVE YOU ENCOUNTERED SIMILAR CHALLENGES?

Describe a personal situation in which students' perceived lack of ability caused them to avoid involvement in particular activities.

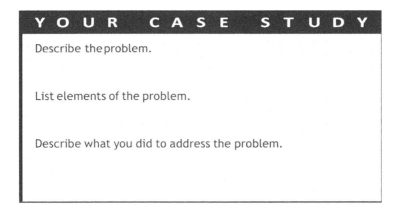

WHAT MIGHT BE THE PROBLEM?

It is believed in Expectancy-Value Theory that individuals must feel some ownership of and control over their successes if they are to be motivated (see Chapter 3 – *Why Should I Do It?*). The motivational importance of such perceived control over one's successes and failures has been made a focus of the work of Bernard Weiner in his *Attribution Theory* (Weiner, 1986, 2018; see also Graham, 2020). The hub of Attribution Theory is that individuals have a desire to explain and interpret their successes and failures by attributing these performances to causes. In other words, individuals ask questions such as 'Why did I fail the exam?,' 'Why did my team lose?' or 'Why did I achieve so well?' It is, however, more likely that these types of questions are asked after failure rather than after success. In answering them individuals attribute their successes and failures to various causes, some of which can be personally controlled, some of which cannot. Depending on the nature of the attribution made, motivation may be enhanced or diminished.

The first element in the mental processing of success or failure on a particular task for the individual is an affective one. When we are told we have failed on something, we are generally flooded with feelings of disappointment and frustration. These affective reactions to the outcome gradually become moderated – weakened or intensified – as the individual begins to attribute the failure to causes. In other words, there may be a change in emotions dependent on the attributions made. The individual who fails in a mathematics test may attribute the failure to lack of preparation. In this instance, the effect on future motivation will be considerably different from that of the individual who attributes the failure to lack of ability. If the failure is attributed to bad luck (e.g., illness), future motivation may or may not be affected; however, if the failure is attributed to task difficulty, the individual may withdraw from involvement in the task in the future.

This process of attribution can also be illustrated with a success example. Most individuals initially feel pleased that they have successfully passed a test or performed an activity. However, the student's perception of the task as very easy and whether the student fluked preparation and was simply lucky will have a considerable impact on further affective feelings and on later motivation. The student might consider that their success was not really in their control (i.e., not related to their effort), so motivation might drop. If, on the other hand, they felt that the task was very easy because they had put a lot of effort into preparation, their motivation would remain high because of pride in their achievement.

Attribution Theory, therefore, rests on three basic assumptions. First, it assumes that people attempt to find out or determine the causes of their own behavior and that of others. In other words, people are motivated to seek out information that helps them make attributions of cause and effect, particularly in situations where the outcome is unexpected or negative. Second, the theory assumes that the reasons that people give to explain their behavior govern their behavior in relatively predictable and consistent ways from one situation to the next: they do not behave randomly. The final assumption is that causes to which particular behavior is used to attribute performance on a task will influence motivational, emotional, and cognitive responses to a subsequent task.

There are four causes that are commonly perceived as the most responsible for students' success and failure: *ability, effort, task difficulty*, and *luck*. Ability refers to how good a person thinks they are in a particular activity: for example, some people feel that they are good at tennis, others at mathematics, others at drama, and so on. Effort refers to how much energy the person puts into a particular task and whether that effort is specific or general, or effective or less effective, to the task.

We have all experienced times when we put a lot of effort into completing a task or achieving a goal. We also have experienced times when we really put in little effort. Task difficulty refers to how difficult the person perceives the task is. Tasks that most people can master are labelled easy, while tasks that few can master are labelled difficult. Finally, luck refers to things that lie outside of personal control that may affect performance (i.e., uncontrollable influences, e.g., being unwell or having a flat tire on the way to an exam).

These perceived 'causes' of success and failure can be considered under our control to different extents. For example, ability may not be under our control while effort and effective strategies are. Perceived causes of performance might also be considered relatively stable or unstable. For example, effort and luck may be unstable, while ability stable, and each may be either generalizable across a range of activities or specific to a particular activity. Each of these dimensions may influence a person's interpretation of the significance of success and failure. The stability dimension affects the individual's expectations of future success or failure on a given task, while whether an individual feels he or she has control affects feelings or self-confidence.

Attributing performance to ability could have a double-edged-sword effect on students' subsequent motivation and performance, and this depends on their view of the malleability of their ability and the role of effort in this (Dweck, 2006, 2017; Dweck & Yeager, 2019; Haimovitz & Dweck, 2017). Some students have a *fixed mindset* of ability and believe that their ability is something that they are born with and is unchangeable (or 'stable'), and there is nothing much they can do to improve it. In this regard, students with a fixed mindset who see their success as a consequence of their ability may become complacent and subsequently put in less effort, believing that they are smart and do not need to exert effort. Similarly, when these students fail on a task and they attribute it to ability, they may subsequently stop trying as they do not believe that the effort they put in will make any difference in their ability which is seen as responsible for their poor task performance.

In contrast, some other students have a *growth mindset* of ability and believe that their ability is changeable (or 'unstable') and, through effort and persistence, they can improve or develop it. In this regard, students with a growth mindset who attribute their success to ability are likely to be more motivated and take up more challenging tasks because they believe that their capacity, which can be developed with effort, enables them to tackle the tasks. When students with a growth mindset attribute their failure to ability, they may likely put in extra effort on subsequent tasks, believing that the effort they put in is likely to lead to the development of ability and, in turn, improvement on task performance. Clearly, it is important that students hold a growth mindset of ability when they make ability attributions of their performance. When students hold a growth mindset, the effects of ability attributions on their motivation are likely to be more similar to those of effort attributions.

What factors are known to influence attributions of achievement? The achievement of others relative to our own is one important factor. For example, if students achieve much the same as others, they are more likely to attribute their success or failure to external causes (e.g., task difficulty).

On the other hand, if an individual's achievement varies from others, and is significantly better or worse, the individual is likely to attribute it to internal factors (e.g., ability or effort). The frames of reference students use to evaluate their achievement and ability can distort reality. For example, students of high ability may consider themselves lacking ability when they are in a high stream or selective class in which many students are achieving as well or better than they are. In other words, these students become little fishes in a big pond (Liem et al., 2013, 2015). In some cases, therefore, selective schools and streamed classes may not be a positive influence on the motivation of students, especially those in a high–ability school or stream.

An individual's history of achievement also affects attributions as it is associated with the stability dimension. In other words, outcomes that are consistent with previous patterns are likely to be attributed to stable causes (e.g., ability, 'I always fail in reading because I am not smart'). Outcomes that run counter to previous patterns are likely to be attributed to unstable causes (e.g., effort or luck).

Positive or negative beliefs about ability also influence causal attributions. Individuals who believe that they are competent and also perform well have this competence confirmed and are likely, therefore, to attribute their success to stable causes (e.g., ability). Students who believe they are competent but fail are likely to question the causes of their failure in terms of unstable causes (e.g., effort or luck). Conversely, students who believe that they lack competence are likely to attribute their successes to unstable causes (e.g., luck), which is consistent with their perception of themselves as incompetent. Teacher's feedback is also important, and we consider this in a later section of this chapter.

What are some characteristics of good attributions? In achievement tasks, it is important that individuals attribute the success or failure in previous tasks to causes that will positively motivate future performance, and not to dysfunctional ones that will discourage further involvement. It has been found that students with adaptive or optimal achievement motivation generally attribute their successes to ability and effort including effective learning strategies, and failures to lack of effort or use of less effective learning strategies. Those with less adaptive achievement motivation generally attribute their successes to external causes (e.g., the ease of the task or luck) and thereby discount the extent that their ability and effort are responsible for their successes. Hence, these students experience less pride for their successful performance. These students also attribute their failures to lack of ability rather than to external factors or to lack of effort.

Weiner suggests that the major differences between individuals high and low in achievement needs are that high-need achievers are more likely to *initiate* achievement activities, work with greater *intensity*, *persist* longer in the face of failure, and *choose* more tasks of intermediate difficulty than are persons low in achievement needs. Among variables that have been found to influence achievement motivation and attributions include sex differences, ethnic differences, achievement needs, self-esteem, emotional state, reinforcement schedules, and internal/external control perceptions. It is therefore important for teachers to find out their students' attribution factors and what these factors mean to their motivation to learn.

How might the attributional beliefs of teachers influence student motivation? The primary focus in Attribution Theory is on an individual's reaction to success or failure in terms of the personal attributions made. As we have discussed above, when an individual's failure is attributed to lack of ability, which is uncontrollable (but recall our discussion on growth mindset above), shame and embarrassment may lead to a decrease in performance. On the other hand, failure attributed to lack of effort, which is controllable, may provoke feelings of guilt in the individual and lead to an increase in performance (see also achievement emotions in Chapter 8 – *How Do I Feel?*). However, Weiner points out that the reaction of the teacher to a student whose failure is perceived to be the result of either lack of ability or lack of effort has significant implications for the student's future motivation for the task.

When teachers perceive that students' failures are due to lack of ability, they often express sympathy and offer no punishment. On the other hand, when teachers perceive that students' failures are due to lack of effort, they often express anger and punish the students (e.g., through verbal reprimands). In the first instance, expressed sympathy and lack of punishment may lead an individual to believe that the teacher ascribes his or her failure to uncontrollable causes like low ability, increasing that individual's personal beliefs about lack of control and responsibility. Shame and reduced performance may be the result. On the other hand, when teachers express anger toward students for exerting insufficient effort, and when that anger is accepted by the students, then there should be increased inferences of self-responsibility which raise guilt and lead to improved performance.

Research certainly tends to support these notions. For example, it appears that teachers give negative feedback to failing students whom they perceive have ability but have not put in sufficient effort, yet give little or sympathetic feedback to students whose ability they doubt. When teachers communicate anger to children following their failure using cues such as loud voice, children tend to ascribe their poor performance to lack of effort. This is subsequently related to high expectation of success and increased performance (see Graham, 2020).

It would appear from this information that communication of anger and punishment for failure will prove more effective in stimulating further motivation to improve performance than sympathetic feedback and the absence of reprimand. This is certainly the case when the teacher perceives that the students are capable of the task. However, this principle should not be accepted without considering qualifying conditions and mitigating circumstances. In particular, as teachers we must be very certain that increased effort will, in fact, lead to improved performance because effort attributions may also lead to negative consequences: in a situation in which a student's increased effort is not followed by better performance on a task, the student may feel that they are not smart and trying hard is futile. It is therefore important to design and assign students optimally challenging tasks that can be successfully completed with effort and persistence. However, persistence in the face of continuous failure in some instances may not be the best approach to achieve long-term success, and it would be beneficial for the learner to alter the direction of his or her energies. In this case, being sympathetic and withholding punishment may be the appropriate methods of producing a change in achievement.

THINGS TO TRY

Research into Attribution Theory indicates that the attributions that an individual makes influence task choice, need for and type of feedback sought, motivation and persistence, and performance outcomes. Success-motivated individuals strive for information about their proficiency and prefer moderately difficult tasks, while failure-avoiding individuals try to avoid such feedback and therefore choose tasks that are too easy or too difficult.

It is important that students attribute their successes and failures to factors that will enhance further motivation. If students attribute failures to stable causes such as ability and task difficulty there is little perceived point in trying again at the task. Indeed, such future efforts will simply confirm the situation and reduce the individual's perceived competence and self-esteem. Generally, you should encourage and teach students, particularly low-achieving students, to attribute their successes and failures to the factors over which they have most control, that is, personal effort or strategy use. In particular, it is important for you to modify students' dysfunctional or less optimal attribution patterns for failure and success. Help students value and accept success that can be attributed to their own ability and effort. Among techniques that have been found valuable are persuasion, providing opportunities for meaningful success experiences, exercises, and demonstrations through role models, and training in appropriate strategy use.

We must caution here about ascribing inappropriate attributions with the intention of improving student motivation. As we mentioned earlier, the attribution to effort can be a double-edged sword. Imagine that Johnny has a perceptual motor problem and his writing is very untidy. He receives feedback from his teacher that he needs to improve and that the best way to do this is by increasing his effort. Johnny puts in more and more effort, to no avail. The teacher says his writing is still very sloppy and he needs to put in more effort and practice. What can Johnny do? In this case, he will probably withdraw from the task and become alienated from writing. In Johnny's case, the poor writing should have been attributed to a motor skill deficiency and the problem addressed through a restructuring of the task or special remedial programs rather than insisting on more effort.

Teachers often inappropriately ascribe poor performance to a student's supposed lack of ability. For example, teachers may ascribe low ability to a student in mathematics when, with a redesigning of tasks so that they are more appropriate to the student's capacity, along with increased effort on the part of the student, success can be achieved. At times, situations need to be restructured so that individuals see the link between effort and success. The experience of success alone may be sufficient to effect positive changes to learning motives and strategies, and may be the most important factor in promoting positive emotional responses. These feelings may, in their turn, result in alterations to behavior designed to increase the probability of further success.

Research indicates one interesting cross-over effect of ability and effort relating to self-esteem. Younger children generally equate ability and effort. In other words, they believe bright kids work hard, dumb kids loaf. Adolescents, however, are likely to maintain that if students are putting in a lot of effort, then they are probably not so bright. In their view, students with a lot of ability appear to achieve success effortlessly. A lot of adolescents go to a great deal of trouble covering up the effort they put into achieving success. It is not unusual for even university students to be dismissive of any effort they have put into exam preparation. Perhaps you have heard students bemoaning their lack of preparation for an upcoming test, while in reality they have secretly studied very hard. This might also, of course, be an example of a failure-avoiding strategy. The relationship between ability and effort is not straightforward. In a society in which the value of hard work and diligence is strongly socialized by parents and teachers and becomes a cultural norm, students believe that putting in effort and being persistent in what one does is a noble quality and may even improve their brightness. In other words, these students believe that, regardless of their perceived ability, they should put in a lot of effort and be determined in their studies.

In much of what we have said above, we have suggested that children should be guided by teachers toward a belief in themselves as constructive forces influencing their own successes and failures in the classroom. To the extent that students believe their successes and failures are subject to external forces (e.g., the teacher setting easy or hard tasks), or that their successes and failures are a matter of luck, they are acting as *pawns* (De Charms, 1984), rather like in a game of chess. In other words, they feel powerless and ineffective in their studies. To the extent that this feeling of powerlessness generalizes to a range of behaviors, students may become learned helpless. In other words, they lose the capacity to be accountable for their own behavior and performance and learn to be helpless (and hopeless!). On the other hand, students who seize the initiative, perceive the relationship between success and effort, restructure situations to maximize chances for success in so far as circumstances permit, and have a realistic view of their abilities, are *origins*. These are students with a strong sense of agency.

According to De Charms (1984), the two dimensions, origin and pawn, lie along a continuum: individuals are neither one nor the other exclusively. In different situations, students may be more like origins, while in others they may be pawns. Some students, for example, are very much pawns in the classroom, while origins on the sporting field. These differences may also be observed within the same student across different subjects.

Students are not born as an origin or a pawn. They develop these statuses through socialization in various circumstances. Teachers can act as effective agents in developing origin characteristics in students. Where motivation to achieve is severely lacking, *attributional retraining* has been shown to be very successful. The essence of attributional retraining is to train individuals to change their patterns of attribution so that lack of motivation, perceived lack of self-efficacy, and perceived states of learned helplessness are reduced. Encouraging students to attribute their poor performance to temporary causes such as lack of effort or inappropriate strategy use, over which they have control, should increase their expectations of future performance, reduce anxiety and fear of failure, alleviate feelings of helplessness, and lead to better motivation and task performance in later activities. Furthermore, particularly for failure-accepting students, it is important to teach them to accept credit for success rather than to concentrate only on training them to substitute lack of effort attribution for inability attribution following failure.

It is important that you acknowledge positive effort rather than always emphasizing lack of effort, which can be counterproductive. It is useful, for example, to comment, when appropriate, that you can see that the students are putting a lot of effort into their work, and associate this effort with the resultant better achievement. You can also comment, with good effect, on the attitude of students, for example, by commenting on their thoughtfulness and the interest they are showing in their work.

QUESTION POINTS

?	Success and failure are both important motivating experiences. How can teachers use these to maximize motivation in the classroom? What might be the effects of repeated success and repeated failure on self-concept and level of aspiration?
?	Think about your own attributions for success and failure. Do you emphasize an internal or an external attribution factor? How do these attributions influence your subsequent motivation?

ACTION STATIONS

* Get to know the attributions that your students make for their successes and failures. After giving feedback on particular assignments and tests, ask students why they got the mark they did. Repeat this over several pieces of work and ascertain whether there are any patterns in the responses given. In particular, pay attention to students whom you have seen as task-oriented or failure-avoiding. Also, relate this information about your students' attributions to the level of motivation you perceive particular students showing for the task at hand.

- Do you think that attributional retraining is needed for particular students? Develop a plan for attributional training that you could use with your students. Implement and monitor the plan. Target specific students and observe its effect on them.
- Revisit your personal case study and describe your new insights and solutions after reading this chapter.

REFERENCES AND RECOMMENDED READINGS

Amemiya, J., & Wang, M. T. (2018). Why effort praise can backfire in adolescence. *Child Development Perspectives, 12*, 199–203.

Dean, K., & Koenig, A. (2019). Cross-cultural differences and similarities in attribution. In K. Keith (Ed.). *Cross-cultural psychology: Contemporary themes and perspectives* (2nd ed., pp. 575–597). New York, NY: John Wiley.

De Charms, R. (1984). Motivation and enhancement in educational settings. In R. Ames & C. Ames (Eds.), *Research on motivation in education: Vol.1. Student motivation.* Orlando, FL: Academic Press.

Dweck, C. S. (2006). *Mindset: The new psychology of success.* New York, NY: Ballantine Books.

Dweck, C. S. (2017). The journey to children's mindsets – and beyond. *Child Development Perspectives, 11*, 139–144.

Dweck, C. S., & Yeager, D. S. (2019). Mindsets: A view from two eras. *Perspectives on Psychological Science, 14*, 481–496.

Graham, S. (2020). An attributional theory of motivation. *Contemporary Educational Psychology, 61*, 101861.

Graham, S. (2016). An attributional perspective on motivation in ethnic minority youth. In J. DeCuir-Gunby, & P. Schutz (Eds.), *Researching race and ethnicity in the study of teaching, learning, and motivation in educational contexts.* New York, NY: Routledge.

Graham, S., & Taylor, A. Z. (2016). Attribution theory and motivation in school. In K. R. Wentzel, & D. B. Miele (Eds.). *Handbook of motivation at school* (pp. 11–33). New York, NY: Routledge.

Haimovitz, K., & Dweck, C. S. (2017). The origins of children's growth and fixed mindsets: New research and a new proposal. *Child Development, 88*, 1849–1859.

Liem, G. A. D., Marsh, H. W., Martin, A. J., McInerney, D. M., & Yeung, A. S. (2013). The big-fish-little-pond effect and a national policy of within-school ability streaming: Alternative frames of reference. *American Educational Research Journal, 50*, 326–370.

Liem, G. A. D., McInerney, D. M., & Yeung, A. S. (2015). Academic self-concept in ability streams: Considering the role of domain specificity and same-stream peers. *Journal of Experimental Education, 83*, 83–109.

Perry, R., & Hamm, J. (2017). An attribution perspective on competence and motivation. In A. J. Elliot, C. S. Dweck, & D. S. Yeager, (Eds.), *Handbook of competence and motivation* (2nd ed., pp. 61–84). New York, NY: Guilford.

Schwinger, M., Wirthwein, L., Lemmer, G., & Steinmayr, R. (2014). Academic self-handicapping and achievement: A meta-analysis. *Journal of Educational Psychology, 106*, 744–761.

Stewart, T. L. H., Clifton, R. A., Daniels, L. M., Perry, R. P., Chipperfield, J. G., & Ruthig, J. C. (2011). Attributional retraining: Reducing the likelihood of failure. *Social Psychology of Education, 14*, 75–92

Török, L., Szabó, Z. P., & Tóth, L. (2018). A critical review of the literature on academic self-handicapping: Theory, manifestations, prevention and measurement. *Social Psychology of Education, 5*, 1175–1202.

Weiner, B. (1986). *An attributional theory of motivation and emotion.* New York, NY: Springer-Verlag.

Weiner, B. (2010). The development of an attribution-based theory of motivation: A history of ideas. *Educational Psychologist, 45*, 28–36.

Weiner, B. (2018). The legacy of an attributional approach to motivation and emotion: A no-crisis zone. *Motivation Science, 4*, 4–14.

5 I BELIEVE I CAN DO IT

'I don't know! I can't do it!' muttered Peter as he wrestled with figuring out the difference between similes and metaphors and finding examples for each.

Overhearing Peter's murmurs, Mr. Davis asked Peter if he would like to work with two other students who were working on the same task. He commented, 'You and the group might work together and find the answer. I am sure you'll be able to do. Here is a list of examples to help you find the answer.'

After ten minutes, Peter and his group beamed with delight as they could not wait to give Mr. Davis their answer and present their own examples of the two figurative expressions.

How confident one feels about one's ability in a given activity influences the commitment and the amount of energy one brings to the task. We have all

DOI: 10.4324/9781003198383-6

come across individuals who lack confidence, run themselves down, believe that they have little autonomy in what they do, lack personal control, responsibility and self-determination, and avoid decision making. These individuals may also lack self-awareness and self-understanding, and appear not to be able to manage their learning at all well. This is expressed in unmotivated behavior characterized by poor planning and time management, poor goal-setting, poor use of learning strategies, and low rate of work completion.

HAVE YOU ENCOUNTERED SIMILAR CHALLENGES?

Describe a personal situation in which your students were not able to manage their learning, mainly due to a lack of confidence.

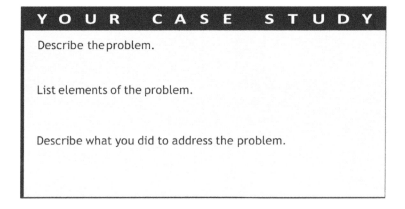

YOUR   CASE   STUDY

Describe the problem.

List elements of the problem.

Describe what you did to address the problem.

WHAT MIGHT BE THE PROBLEM?

According to Social-Cognitive Theory, motivation is a function of personal expectations and goals, and self-evaluative processes. As people work to achieve goals, they evaluate their progress too. If the evaluation is positive, personal feelings of *self-efficacy* are enhanced, which sustain motivation. Self-efficacy refers to self-perceptions or beliefs of capability to learn and perform particular tasks at particular levels. Efficacy beliefs influence how people feel, think, motivate themselves, and behave. Social and contextual factors affect motivation through their influence on expectations, goals, and self-evaluations of progress. Among the socio-contextual factors that have an impact are social comparisons, rewards and reinforcement, classroom organization, and types of feedback.

Albert Bandura (1986, 1997, 2001, 2019) believes that students' beliefs in their efficacy to regulate their own learning and to master academic activities determine their aspirations, levels of motivation, and academic achievements. Bandura also believes that the higher people's perceived self-efficacy, the higher the goals or challenges they set for themselves and the firmer their commitment to them. It is believed that children base their appraisals of ability on a wide range of sources including their performance, feedback from others, as well as vicarious (observational) experiences such as seeing others being praised, ignored or ridiculed for performing in a like manner. High self-efficacy for a particular activity does not necessarily lead to motivated behavior in and of itself. As we discussed in Chapter 3 (*Why Should I Do It?*), the perceived value of the activity and expectations of the outcome also influence the level of motivation. However, without a sense of self-efficacy, it is unlikely that learners will engage in activities, irrespective of whether they are perceived as important or not. Teachers' beliefs in their personal efficacy to motivate and promote learning also affect the types of learning environments they create and the level of academic progress their students achieve.

THINGS TO TRY

Motivated learners set learning goals for themselves, use a range of strategies purposefully, monitor their own learning, and adapt their strategies as required. How can educators help students develop self-efficacy? Among the important ways to help develop and maintain self-efficacy among students are by providing opportunities for students to make decisions and to have some control over the learning process; allowing students opportunities to develop autonomy and self-determination in their learning; challenging students to take personal responsibility for their learning and to be actively involved in their learning experiences; teaching planning, goal-setting skills, and information-processing or cognitive strategies; as well as using role models and providing attributional feedback.

As part of this process, you need to have students confront their negative thoughts about their own capacity to be successful in particular activities. Students should consider their thoughts and feelings and how they relate to their behavior. The quality of the relationship set up between you and the students is very important in this process. If you show genuine care for the students, you will have a great chance of setting up an optimal learning environment.

Providing opportunities for students to make decisions and to have some control over their learning means realistically considering those things that students may have some control over. These include the type of activity, the level of mastery, the time taken, the nature of the assessment (which could include self-assessment), the type of reward, and any social involvement that the activity might include, such as peer group work.

The setting of challenging but attainable goals and the achievement of these goals enhances self-efficacy and motivation. Teachers need to assist students to set both short-term and long-term goals. Among techniques that teachers use are setting upper and lower limits on students' goals and removing them when students understand the nature of the task and their immediate capabilities, and using games such as shooting for goals in basketball. Goal-setting conferences where students learn to assess goal difficulty and present skills in collaboration with the teacher are also useful. As students become more self-regulated, they will be more adept at setting their own goals. Short-term goals are important, particularly for younger or novice learners, as progress is more noticeable. However, the achievement of long-term goals is ultimately more important for the development of self-efficacy as it offers more information about developed capabilities. It is also important to remind students to set not only *outcome-oriented* goals (i.e., performance on a task, e.g., attaining 80% of the answers correct in the upcoming test) but also *process-oriented* goals (i.e., steps and strategies to accomplish the task or outcome goal, e.g., spending two hours a day on the practice problems). Focusing on process goals is as important as, if not more important than, setting outcome goals.

Further, teaching students good planning skills is essential as good planning involves a capacity for self-monitoring, that is, recognizing one's intellectual strengths and weaknesses and preferred ways of thinking. When planning, students should be taught how to accommodate their strengths and weaknesses and think out the time necessary and steps needed to accomplish their tasks.

If students are taught how to learn and monitor their learning progress (i.e., if their metacognitive and meta-learning skills are developed), they are more likely to feel competent in a range of learning situations and, therefore, more motivated to continue in these activities. Both teachers and peers may also be used to demonstrate that particular tasks lie within the range of ability of particular students. Observing others succeed can convey to observers that they too are capable and can motivate them to attempt the task, especially when the students being observed have similar characteristics to the observers.

We need to encourage learners to see the relationship between ability, effort, and success, and in particular to encourage them to attribute their failures to factors over which they have some control. When a student feels in control, motivation is enhanced. In this context, it is worthwhile remembering that this sense of control as a function of effort may come from mastering strategies for learning and solving problems. Indeed, even in the face of failure, attributing future outcomes to effort can encourage a child to try again. At other times, attributing success to ability enhances self-efficacy and motivation. This has important implications for students with learning disabilities who may develop a sense of helplessness with regard to their lack of ability relative to others.

In order to enhance self-efficacy, feedback should also emphasize goals achieved or gains made rather than shortfalls in performance. This can be done, for example, by emphasizing progress: we can tell students that they have achieved 75% or we can highlight the 25% shortfall in their performance. Accenting the gains enhances perceived self-efficacy while highlighting deficiencies undermines self-regulatory influences with a resultant deterioration in student performance.

Probably the most important source of feedback for younger students is the teacher. As students become more self-regulated, they will evaluate their performance themselves in terms of their perceived ability and effort and the appropriateness of particular goals, modifying their involvement accordingly. Under these circumstances, motivation is channeled into achieving goals that are perceived as attainable and worthwhile.

Feelings of self-confidence are very motivating to students who have not enjoyed many successes in school. Students are more likely to take responsibility for their learning when they realize that they can achieve on their own. Finally, rewards may be used to indicate that a goal has been achieved and hence enhance self-efficacy and motivation. The strengths and weaknesses of reward use will be discussed in Chapter 6 (*Stars, Stamps, and Jelly Beans*).

Modeling Self-Efficacy

Teachers are highly influential models in establishing and maintaining students' attitudes toward their studies. In order to influence students positively, teachers should show the value of the learning process and learning tasks by modeling an interest in these; model excitement and enthusiasm; model expertise, for example, through use of worked examples; model thought processes, self-monitoring, and metacognitive strategies; model setting goals, time management, planning, and self-evaluation.

In order to enhance the success of students, you should apply the following principles in learning and teaching sequences:

- focus attention on a specific area or task and ensure that competing demands are reduced or eliminated;
- give a general orientation or overview – explain what is to happen;
- label verbally and visually any new concepts or objects, and have students repeat them;
- verbalize thought processes involved in problem-solving or performing behaviors;
- demonstrate methods of gathering information so that students can learn these cognitive and learning strategies themselves;
- proceed step by step – break each complex activity into smaller operations and demonstrate processes by thinking aloud;
- perform actions with an appropriate pace to maintain attention;
- provide student opportunity for guided practice, e.g., through teacher mentoring or peer-tutoring so that corrective feedback by you can be given;

- provide opportunities for focused attention and practice;
- do not emphasize mistakes – redemonstrate and encourage another attempt;
- provide effective reinforcement and feedback for efforts and achievements;
- show links between goals, practice, and payoff;
- use exemplars to demonstrate behaviors, skills, and attitudes.

Implied in this approach is the notion that *you are teaching students how to learn.* If students perceive that you are showing them how to learn, they are more likely to be motivated to learn. Finally, you should provide a performance context in which outcomes, personal goals, and a sense of self-efficacy are mutually valued by teacher and student.

Peer Models and Self-Efficacy

Self-regulation and self-efficacy have to be seen in their social context. This may include social assistance, peer mentoring, and other sources of support. Students are equally inclined to replicate the behavior of peers or adults, according to two criteria. First, the behavior must appear to be instrumental in achieving goals. Second, the person performing the behavior must appear competent. In the case where peers are viewed as equally competent as adults, the behavior of the peers is likely to be replicated. When students question the competence of peers, they tend to replicate the behavior of adults. When same-sex peers are viewed as less competent than younger peers, students pattern their behavior after the competent but younger peers rather than similar-age mates of lower competence than themselves. Thus, as important as characteristic similarities between a student and his or her peer models are, the student must also have the confidence in the models.

Peers may be effectively used to demonstrate classroom procedures. The motivational effects of these demonstrations are hypothesized to depend, in part, on perceptions of self-efficacy, or personal beliefs about one's capability to perform the desired behavior to the same level of proficiency as demonstrated.

Teachers often use peer modeling for a variety of purposes. One common use is to illustrate how activities should not be sex-stereotyped: thus, we have girls and boys alike emptying the school bins, learning bush dancing, and doing cross-stitch and embroidery. Observational learning principles and, in particular, peer modeling are used with students who experience various forms of social anxiety such as social withdrawal and isolation. Typically, the isolate is required to observe peers engage in the requisite behavior. This process may be achieved through the use of live or video models. For example, we can present students with a film depicting several peer models engaging in a variety of social activities that we want them to learn.

One important aspect of peer models is that they may supply a realistic gauge of what is potentially possible for children who lack a sense of self-efficacy. Adults may be perceived as possessing a level of competence that children are unlikely to attain. In this latter case, peer models may be more successful.

Same-sex models do not appear to be any more successful than different-sex models except in those behaviors that relate to gender-appropriate behavior. Thus, the sex of the model seems less important in general learning contexts.

Students can be encouraged to make diaries to monitor their work habits and how these habits relate to the performance achieved. In these diaries, students could also be asked to draw or write a description of a new idea or procedure to show that they understand what to do. These can be reviewed by the teacher and student to ascertain where cognitive motivational links are made as the child is learning. Students should also be encouraged to check to see if they understand what is to be done and to ask questions if they are unclear; talk out loud and describe what they are doing or thinking while they are working out a solution or doing an activity; copy the teacher or other students who show good ways to find information; and practice what they have been shown and try again if they make a mistake, thinking about how they can break down a large piece of work into a series of small ones. Peer modeling can be used effectively to teach these behaviors.

Students should also be encouraged to observe what happens to other students when they do a task or solve problems. Do they get rewards or feel good about themselves? They should also be encouraged to think about what might encourage them to work hard on a task.

Self-Management and Self-Regulated Learning

Even within a behaviorally oriented classroom, learners may still be involved in goal setting, monitoring their own work, keeping progress records, and evaluating their work. They may also be involved in selecting their own rewards and punishments and administering them. Obviously, the developmental level of the learners has much to do with the successful implementation of such a plan. The ability of students to set goals is very important to self-management and motivation. Students who successfully set clear and realistic goals and can communicate them to others (e.g., the teacher) perform better than those who have vague goals. With appropriate training, students can monitor their own work and keep progress records that should also foster their motivation to learn. They can also be taught to evaluate their own work adequately, although monitoring by the teacher is important to validate the accuracy of the evaluation. Self-reinforcement is the final step in self-management. Bandura argues that giving oneself rewards on the basis of good performance enhances future performance. Other psychologists, however, maintain that it is unnecessary.

Based on Social-Cognitive Theory, Barry Zimmerman, Timothy Cleary, and their colleagues (Cleary, 2018; Cleary & Zimmerman, 2004; Cleary & Kitsantas, 2017; Zimmerman, 2002) have developed the *self-regulated learning* approach to teaching and learning. In this approach, self-regulated learners view learning as a systematic and controllable process, and they accept responsibility for their achievement outcomes. Self-regulated learners approach tasks with confidence, diligence, and resourcefulness. They proactively seek out information when needed, attempting to take the necessary steps to master it. Self-regulated students are metacognitively, motivationally, and behaviorally active learners in their own learning. In terms of metacognitive processes, self-regulated learners plan, set goals, organize, self-monitor, and evaluate themselves at various points during the learning process. Because of this, they are self-aware, knowledgeable, and decisive in their approach to learning. Self-regulated learners appear to be self-motivated and report high self-efficacy (i.e., a high belief in themselves as learners), self-agentic (i.e., they accept responsibility for successes and failures), as well as valuing the importance of effort. They also show intrinsic interest in the task.

Self-regulated learning may be domain-specific. This means that learners who have learned to regulate themselves in a particular activity such as reading may need to learn self-regulation in another activity such as essay writing. The skills of self-regulation detailed above do not occur naturally or spontaneously in learners. Indeed, the development of such skills is complex and gradual in nature. Teaching episodes need to be developed to encourage learners to develop these skills across a range of subjects so that, in the long term, self-regulating becomes a generalized capacity.

QUESTION POINTS

?	What do you say and do when a student says 'I can't do this'? What features of the individual and situation do you take into account?
?	What expectations do you hold of students in your class? How might these expectations influence your treatment of the students? What impact might this have on their motivation to learn?
?	How self-regulated do you think you are as a teacher? What will you do to be a more self-regulated teacher and model this to your students in the classroom?

ACTION STATIONS

- Reflect on how you teach and project your confidence in your students. How do you think your students would judge your ability to make them feel confident about succeeding in your class? How could you improve on this?
- Interview teachers about learned helplessness in students. How might teachers inadvertently contribute to this condition? What practices could you implement to alleviate learned helplessness in your students?
- Develop a plan to support autonomy in your students while minimizing your control. Implement this plan and monitor its effects. What effect

does it have on student motivation? Does this vary according to particular students, or to particular classes?
- Revisit your personal case study and describe your new insights and solutions after reading this chapter.

REFERENCES AND RECOMMENDED READINGS

Ahn, H. S., Usher, E. L., Butz, A., & Bong, M. (2016). Cultural differences in the understanding of modelling and feedback as sources of self-efficacy information. *British Journal of Educational Psychology, 86*, 112–136.

Bandura, A. (1986). *Social foundations of thought and action*. Englewood Cliffs, NJ: Prentice Hall.

Bandura, A. (1997). *Self-efficacy: The exercise of control*. New York, NY: Freeman.

Bandura, A. (2001). Social-cognitive theory: An agentic perspective. *Annual Review of Psychology, 52*,1–26.

Bandura, A. (2019). Applying theory for human betterment. *Perspectives on Psychological Science, 14*, 12–15.

Bjork, R. A., Dunlosky, J., & Kornell, N. (2013). Self-regulated learning: Beliefs, techniques, and illusions. *Annual Review of Psychology, 64*, 417–444.

Brier, N. (2010). *Self-regulated learning: Practical interventions for struggling teens*. Champaign, IL: Research Press.

Cash, R. M. (2016). *Self-regulation in the classroom: Helping students learn how to learn*. Golden Valley, MN: Free Spirit Pub.

Cleary, T. J. (Ed.). (2015). *Self-regulated learning interventions with at-risk youth: Enhancing adaptability, performance, and well-being*. Washington, DC: American Psychological Association.

Cleary, T. J. (2018). *The self-regulated learning guide: Teaching students to think in the language of strategies*. New York, NY: Routledge.

Cleary, T. J., & Kitsantas, A. (2017). Motivation and self-regulated learning influences on middle school mathematics achievement. *School Psychology Review, 46*, 88–107.

Cleary, T. J., & Zimmerman, B. J. (2004). Self-regulation empowerment program: A school-based program to enhance self-regulated and self-motivated cycles of student learning. *Psychology in the Schools, 41*, 537–550.

Usher, E. L., & Weidner, B. L. (2018). Sociocultural influences on self-efficacy development. In G. A. D. Liem, & D. M. McInerney (Eds.). *Big theories revisited 2* (pp. 141–164). Charlotte, NC: Information Age Publishing.

Wrosch, C., & Scheier, M. F. (2020). Adaptive self-regulation, subjective well-being, and physical health: The importance of goal adjustment capacities. In A. J. Elliot (Ed.), *Advances in motivation science* (Vol. 7, pp. 199–238). New York, NY: Elsevier.

Zepeda, C. D., Richey, J. E., Ronevich, P., & Nokes-Malach, T. J. (2015). Direct instruction of metacognition benefits adolescent science learning, transfer, and motivation: An in-vivo study. *Journal of Educational Psychology, 107*, 954–970.

Zimmerman, B. J. (2002). Becoming a self-regulated learner: An overview. *Theory into Practice, 41*, 64–70.

Zimmerman, B. J., & Schunk, D. H. (Eds.) (2011). *Handbook of self-regulation of learning and performance*. New York, NY: Taylor & Francis.

6 STARS, STAMPS, AND JELLY BEANS

Mr. Clarke's Year-3 class was sitting around the computer keyboard as Robbie had his turn to use the mouse to trace a pattern presented on the screen. Each child was taking a turn carrying out the instructions. Mr. Clarke noticed that Bob's attention was wandering and that he was fidgeting with the shoe-laces of the kid next to him. Mr. Clarke then said to Madeleine, who was also nearby and waiting her turn, 'Madeleine, good girl, you are paying attention. You must want the next turn.' Madeleine sat up even straighter.

Madeleine proceeded to have her turn. This caught Bob's eye and he quickly sat up and began to pay attention.

Mr. Clarke immediately commented, 'Bob, I'm glad that you are paying attention now. You'll have the next turn.'

DOI: 10.4324/9781003198383-7

Many students appear bored with their work and only make a half-hearted effort at engagement. Many students complain that their work is too hard, too much, or too complex. Students complain that they are not given effective guidance on how to do their work, or receive poor feedback on work completed. How many of us have sat in classrooms where our good behavior or good work has apparently gone unnoticed or ignored by the teacher? How many students have decided that it really isn't worth the effort if they are not getting appropriate feedback or reinforcement? These factors obviously impact on student motivation for learning.

HAVE YOU ENCOUNTERED SIMILAR CHALLENGES?

Before we commence our analysis of unmotivated learning behavior, consider a personal case study that you find relevant.

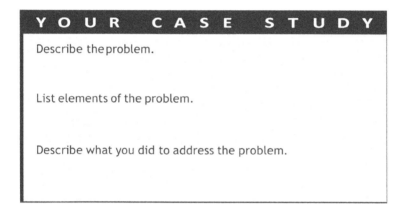

YOUR CASE STUDY

Describe the problem.

List elements of the problem.

Describe what you did to address the problem.

WHAT MIGHT BE THE PROBLEM?

Many students who appear unmotivated by learning tasks become involved when teachers structure the work more effectively and apply rewards to the students' completed work. Indeed, many teachers believe that students are most motivated and work best when they are 'reinforced' in these ways. Reinforcement appears to direct attention to the task at hand and maintain attention, particularly in tasks in which students do not feel competent or interested.

Some time ago, I (Dennis) was sitting in a Sea World presentation in San Diego. On this occasion, the presenter was demonstrating how dolphins could be taught quite complex behavior through a process of shaping in which progressive attempts by the dolphin to perform the desired behavior were rewarded. As the presenter described the procedures involved, I could not help but compare them with procedures used by many teachers in the classroom to shape student cognitive and social behavior. These approaches to teaching are based on two simple principles found to be very successful in training animals. One of these principles relates to programming, conditioning, or shaping behavior, and the other to reinforcing desired behavior. In general, Burrhus Skinner (1971), the originator of what has become known as the Behavioral approach to teaching and learning by offering the Operant Conditioning model of behavior, maintained that all animals, including humans, learn things by having certain aspects of behavior reinforced while other aspects are not. Reinforcement occurs when something is added to the situation that makes the performance of the behavior more likely to occur in the future.

Early studies on the effectiveness of Operant Conditioning were conducted with animals. To train an animal such as a rat or a pigeon, Skinner devised an apparatus now called a Skinner Box. The Skinner Box enables the animal's behavior to be observed and controlled so that particular behaviors are more likely to occur. When these behavioral units, called *operants*, are performed, they are reinforced immediately by the application of a reward such as food. By progressively reinforcing operants that come closer to the goal behavior (a process called *shaping*), the animal is gradually taught to perform quite complex behavior. In the initial stages of conditioning, each time an animal turns into the direction of a lever or a button and moves closer to the lever or the button, the animal is rewarded with food. This is called *continuous reinforcement*. When this response is established, further reinforcement only occurs when the animal adds to the response (e.g., by pressing the lever or pecking the button).

Over a number of trials, the animal builds on and progressively acquires the desired end behavior. At this point, reinforcement is moved to an intermittent schedule and secondary reinforcers such as lights and buzzers may be introduced to facilitate behavior when primary reinforcers are no longer effective (even rats become satiated with food pellets!). Intermittent reinforcement may be presented in a fixed ratio, that is after a specific number of responses; at a fixed interval, after a specific period of time when a response occurs; or at a variable interval, at any time subsequent to a correct response. In general, continuous reinforcement is necessary to establish responses. Once the desired response is established, an intermittent schedule enhances the retention of behavior.

It is important that the target behavior is unpacked into those components that can be sequenced and successively reinforced. The complex behavior of dolphins at the Sea World is not conditioned in one go, but is the result of many hours of laborious training. Furthermore, unless the acquired responses are reinforced intermittently, the behavior will fade and ultimately be extinguished.

Similar results of training may be achieved using negative reinforcement. For example, the floor of the Skinner Box may be mildly electrified. On the performance of the appropriate operant, the current is turned off. A bright rat would very quickly learn to sit on the lever! In general, positive reinforcement is found to be more effective than negative ones that require the animal to avoid deleterious side effects.

Each of the principles of Behaviorism (i.e., reinforcement, shaping, and fading) can be applied effectively in human learning environments. Skinner believed that learning in traditional classrooms was dominated by children trying to avoid unpleasant situations and negative reinforcement such as punishment, rather than working for pleasant rewards. He also believed that there was too great a lapse of time between the performance of particular behavior and its reinforcement. In fact, Skinner believed that reinforcement of desired behavior occurred much too infrequently and erratically. Furthermore, learning episodes were not sufficiently goal-directed in the sense that teachers did not adequately define the behavior desired as goals, nor establish the steps that children needed to progress through in order to achieve these goals.

THINGS TO TRY

As we mentioned above, two principles underpin the use of behavioral techniques in the classroom, both of which can have a positive motivational impact on the learner. The first principle is programming instruction into steps that the student can manage successfully. These steps should build on one another so that a sequence of more complex behavior gradually progresses. Students should never be placed in a situation where success at each successive step in the behavior sequence is not guaranteed. Continuing success is motivational. It builds the momentum for students to carry on.

Students should also be placed in situations where particular forms of behavior are facilitated. For example, if you wish to teach mathematics, your students should be put in a situation where mathematical behavior is more likely to occur. In other words, you should surround them with interesting and appropriate mathematical resources. If you wish to teach swimming, then the logical classroom would be the local pool. Many teachers run into the difficulty of trying to motivate behavior in physical situations where inappropriate behavior is more likely to be motivated. Hence, there is a strong argument for specialized resource rooms. You should also give students immediate feedback on how they are going. This meaningful and well-directed feedback is motivational.

The second principle is the application of reinforcement and punishment to motivate behavior. The application of positive reinforcement builds up a pleasurable association between accomplishing the task and a reward. For children, rewards or reinforcers may be material, such as toys or some enjoyable activity; token, such as stamps, gold stars, or jelly beans; or social, such as the goodwill and recognition of the teacher. Negative reinforcement can also be used. Negative reinforcement creates situations in which the student performs behavior to avoid something unpleasant. A common example of this is staying in one's seat to avoid nagging by the teacher. Often students work hard not because of the inherent interest they have in the task, but to turn off the teacher's nagging!

Positive reinforcement is considered more effective than negative reinforcement. One could construct a classroom so that all the seats of the desks were connected to a mild electric current. When students perform an appropriate behavior, such as putting up their hands before answering a question, the current would be switched off. No doubt the students would 'learn' the behavior very quickly, but perhaps the cost in terms of parental complaints (and escalating electricity bills as a few wayward students persist in not performing the appropriate behavior) would not make it a viable approach! However, the use of negative reinforcement is common, if not quite as extreme. For example, some teachers have students stand up until they respond correctly, after which they are allowed to sit down.

Punishment builds up an unpleasant association between inappropriate behavior, such as non-completion of work, and a noxious event such as detention. Often this style of reinforcement and punishment is called *extrinsic* as it is externally applied, usually by the teacher. If you wish to use extrinsic reinforcement, you need to decide what reinforcers and punishers are appropriate and available for your students.

The important point here is not so much what you think is rewarding or punishing, but rather the effect that it has on the subsequent behavior of your students. A number of studies show that students' opinions about rewards and punishments vary greatly from those of their teachers. There are many examples of things believed by teachers to be positively reinforcing actually being negatively reinforcing or punishing, and examples of things believed by teachers to be punishing actually acting as reinforcers and establishing behavior. Among some of these controlling or punishing strategies that teachers use are nagging, scolding, and grumbling. But to the extent teachers have to use these constantly to eradicate behavior, they are not effective, and may in fact be shaping undesirable student behavior such as out-of-seat behavior and talking out of place.

Potential Problems with Reinforcement

With older students, the knowledge that a student is going to receive a reward for completing particular work may 'contaminate' the effect of extrinsic reinforcement and be detrimental to motivation and performance. Students begin to think, 'Am I being given enough stamps?,' 'Why did Johnny get two stamps while I only got one?,' 'Boy! The teacher is going to give us a chocolate bar for finishing this exercise. The exercise must be more difficult than I thought,' 'I'm never going to get the reward, so why try?,' 'This must be a boring exercise because the teacher has to give us a reward for doing it,' 'Is that all I'm going to be given for all of this work?' One student was heard to say with reference to a popular fitness program sponsored by a pizza company, 'If you don't get the reward, the whole thing is a waste of time.' No doubt you can remember yourself saying these exact things. When rewards are stopped, continuing motivation may also stop. Furthermore, if students are given rewards for activities they are already interested in, they may lose interest in the task in and of itself and begin seeing value only in the reward.

On the other hand, almost everyone agrees that giving rewards for activities in which students show little interest or aptitude usually enhances motivation. In this case, the use of verbal rewards (e.g., praise and positive feedback) can be used to help develop interest in the task. When tangible rewards such as gold stars and money are offered, contingent on performance in a task, or are delivered unexpectedly, intrinsic interest already present may be maintained. A problem occurs when the rewards are offered without regard to the level of performance of the student. In this case, when rewards are withdrawn, students demonstrate diminished motivation in the task. Rewards can be offered for work completed, solving problems successfully, or maintaining a predetermined level of performance, without undermining intrinsic motivation. Bernard Weiner believes that the simple theoretical notion that a reward automatically increases the probability of an immediately prior response occurring again does not stand up when applied to human motivation. Weiner (1990, p. 618) summarizes this in the following way:

> ... *if reward is perceived as controlling, then it undermines future effort, whereas reward perceived as positive feedback is motivating... Furthermore, reward for successful completion of an easy task is a cue to the receiver of this feedback that he or she is low in ability, a belief that inhibits activity, whereas reward for successful completion of a difficult task indicates that hard work was expended in conjunction with high ability, a belief that augments motivation. In addition, reward in a competitive setting is based on social comparison information, signaling that one has high ability and is better than others, whereas reward in a cooperative context signals that one has bettered oneself and has tried hard. Hence, it became recognized that reward has quite a variety of meanings and that each connotation can have different motivational implications.*

Nevertheless, extrinsic token rewards such as stamps, gold stars, and certificates are often used successfully to indicate to younger students how well they have performed individually in comparison with others. As such, these rewards state something about the competence of the student, and may function as an effective motivator for further task involvement and striving for excellence in work. Indeed, students may become 'turned on' to the task and not really require further token reinforcement once they have experienced some level of success. Among appropriate rewards for younger students are sweets, small presents, free time, teacher praise, house points, badges, stars, certificates, and a letter home to parents and child saying how well the student had done. For older students, rewards that have been found to be effective are free time and a positive letter home. It appears that involving parents is very important in determining how effective rewards and punishments at school are. However, for the students who don't receive rewards, such a system can lead to a reduction in their sense of competence and a subsequent loss of interest in the task.

Punishment and Learning

Reward and punishment and their relationship to the process of learning have long been the subject of much folklore. We have proverbs enshrining society's attitudes to these control devices: *'Spare the rod, spoil the child'* or *'You win more bees with honey than vinegar.'* Indeed, our societies have vacillated in their attitude toward the use of reward and punishment to encourage the behavior. Through the early stages of mass education, good discipline and motivation were very much associated with severe punishment techniques – belting, starving, stuffing children's mouths with paper, pulling children's hair or ears, shaking, detentions, loss of privileges, and extra assignments. Many of these excesses still continue. In her parenting memoir, *Battle Hymn of the Tiger Mother*, Amy Chua illustrates some of these disciplining techniques.

A more 'enlightened' time saw the demise of some of the more extreme punishment techniques and the rise of the belief that reward is more effective in establishing desirable behavior in children. Punishment was criticized as ineffective, productive of undesirable behavioral traits, immoral, and inhuman. Baby books and psychology textbooks emphasized the use of rewards rather than punishments as the key to effective learning. This change was supported by early Freudian, Behavioral and Social Learning theories.

The relative effectiveness of reinforcement and punishment has been subjected to research. Punishment is defined in this research as the application of something unpleasant (e.g., a sudden clip across the ear for talking out of turn) or the removal of something pleasant (e.g., not allowing to do a favorite activity) to suppress behavior. A large body of research, all of it carried out with children, suggests that punishment for incorrect behavior leads to faster learning than does reinforcement for correct behavior, and a combination of reinforcement and punishment is no better than punishment alone. A possible explanation for this effect may be that reward is generally non-specific, pervasive, and indiscriminate (i.e., associated with the general pleasantness of the teacher to children), while punishment is used most often for specific acts. The behavior (or non-behavior, e.g., non-completion of an exercise) responsible for the punishment is clearly associated with the punishment, and more specific information is communicated to the child by punishment than by reinforcement. One problem, however, with research such as this is the nature of the punishing stimulus that has been used. Typically, the use of punishment has not been like that in real classrooms and may not necessarily reflect the true impact of punishment. Without doubt, however, the evidence against the use of *corporal punishment* is very strong.

One form of punishment that has been found effective is *response cost*. Response cost refers to the loss of positive reinforcers when particular behaviors are not performed. For example, teachers sometimes allocate individuals or groups thirty minutes of free time per day for their own chosen activities. Each time an individual or member of a group misbehaves, a minute is lost. As such, response cost acts as a punishment. One study of the effects of response cost found that the motivational effect of children losing marbles was greater than that of receiving them, even when the number of marbles retained or received by the students was the same! It appears from this study that the withdrawal of positive reinforcers as a method of regulating or controlling behavior is effective for at least three reasons:

1 It generates a weaker emotional effect than does the presentation of something unpleasant and tends to foster and maintain the subject's orientation toward the agents who control the positive reinforcers.
2 There is less recovery of the punished response when the contingency is removed.
3 It is more frequently used in naturalistic settings than punishment.

Parents often use response cost when they tell their children that they will lose particular privileges if they don't behave. This is often found to be more successful than smacking them when they are naughty. Some parents also believe that it is better than giving rewards to children for behaving and finishing their chores, for these behaviors are an expectation and should not be rewarded.

Are There Appropriate Forms of Punishment?

It appears that punishment can be an effective motivational practice for children in particular contexts. It is, however, often criticized as producing too many unpleasant side effects to be really useful in the classroom. For example, punishment communicates more about what not to do than what to do; it may affect the attitude of the student to the teacher and, in some cases, the punished behavior, such as thumb-sucking, pants-wetting, or out-of-seat behavior, becomes more resistant to change. Verbal rebuke and social disapproval that do not attack a person's worth, withdrawal of privileges and material objects and occasional use of mild physical punishment contingent on specific behavior may, however, be valuable aids to motivation and learning. Punishments at the secondary level which students think are effective include the sending home of an unfavorable note to parents complaining about the student's behavior, being put on report and detention, and being sent to the head teacher. Private conversations with teachers (while not necessarily seen as punishment) are also considered very effective. Punishments which students consider less effective are 'being told off' and being sent to another teacher.

It is important for the student to be given an explanation for why a particular behavior is being punished. There should also be consistency in applying the punishment. If the punishing agent is perceived by the student to be a nurturing person, there is less likelihood of negative consequences arising as a result of the punishment. The punishment that is extremely severe, administered randomly so that the relationship between the action and its consequences is not clear, and which is administered by a hostile and rejecting caretaker, is to be avoided.

Whatever the case for punishment, we must be careful not to return to the bad old days when barbaric forms of retribution were exerted on children. In those days, many thousands of children were subjected to cruelty under laws that were defended, at least in part, by research evidence that punishment can change behavior. One apparent and unfortunate side effect of the use of corporal punishment in schools is that children subjected to it appear to become more tolerant and supportive of its use – surely not a good sign for socializing individuals as caring and loving parents, teachers, and colleagues.

More Programmatic Approaches to Behavioral Teaching

Some more programmatic approaches to behavioral teaching that you might try, found to be very successful in motivating students are the following: *Positive Teaching, Applied Behavior Analysis* (sometimes called *Behavior Modification*), *Precision Teaching*, and *Direct Instruction*.

Positive Teaching. The basis of Positive Teaching is for teachers to identify what students find rewarding and then to structure the teaching environment so as to make such rewards dependent on both the social and academic behavior that they want to encourage. As we stated earlier, teachers have a great deal of control over many of the consequences they provide for their pupils, but few use them consistently and well. Positive Teaching shows teachers how to use behavioral techniques such as shaping, fading, and reinforcement consistently and effectively.

Applied Behavior Analysis. The conditioning of socially appropriate behavior through the use of reinforcement and punishment has been used very successfully in the modification of human behavior. This has particularly been in cases where the behavior is very atypical and resistant to other forms of modification, such as aggression in the class, daydreaming and inattention, out-of-seat behavior, and antisocial conduct, such as spitting and verbal abuse. Recent applications of this technique have been extensively used in special education settings.

To use this approach successfully, you need to *specify the nature of the behavior desired* in behavioral terms – for example, the child will spend more work time at his or her desk; *set a level of behavior* which will be the goal – for example, the child will work for twenty minutes at a time without leaving his or her desk; *instigate an effective reward keeping procedure*, and *assess the behavior* through direct observation such as counting how often it occurs. This form of teaching is often called *Precision Teaching* and may involve the use of stop watches, graphs, and charts. You need to work out the appropriate reinforcing strategies by specifying the award of tokens for the performance of the appropriate behavior, for example, 20 tokens being redeemable for a reward (e.g., lolly or free activity).

Time Out. Time out is a form of reinforcement used to reduce unwanted behavior. In Time Out, students may be removed to a room (or part of the classroom) where they cannot participate in the ongoing activities, nor be distracted by occurrences around them. The theory is that the withdrawal of positive consequences will encourage the student to choose to behave in order to be returned to the more rewarding environment of the classroom. As with all behavioral approaches, behavior modification must be a carefully planned program designed to lead the students to a predetermined goal through the use of rewards. If you are going to practice behavioral techniques, you must set up a situation that allows students to experience good behavior, discriminate between acceptable and unacceptable behavior, and associate his or her appropriate behavior with rewards. You also need to praise students on how well they are doing when the agreed upon reward is presented. Particularly important is the need to help students to become progressively less dependent on the extrinsic reward and to function in the regular classroom as well as in other settings.

Direct Instruction. Direct Instruction is a general term that has acquired a number of different meanings referring to somewhat different instructional practices found to be quite successful in keeping students on-task, engaged, and motivated. What each of these Direct Instruction approaches has in common, however, is a *teacher-centered control of presentation* and *evaluation of learning material.*

Direct Instruction as a Teaching Procedure

One form of Direct Instruction, based on behavioral principles, is a systematic, tasks-analyzed teaching procedure. Three examples of this approach to Direct Instruction have been used widely: the *Direct Instruction System in Arithmetic and Reading (DISTAR)*, *Morphographic Spelling,* and *Corrective Reading.* Research indicates that these direct methods of instruction can be quite effective with a broad range of students. However, the approach generates as much heat as light where academics and teachers argue over the merits of a system that appears to guarantee student success but is extremely teacher-centered and content-dominated. More detailed information about this instructional method can be found on the National Institute for Direct Instruction (NIFDI) website (www.nifdi.org). Key elements of this approach are essentially as follows:

*   developing an explicit step-by-step strategy;
*   ensuring mastery at each step in the process;

- providing specific corrections for student errors;
- gradually fading teacher-directed activities toward independent student work;
- providing adequate and systematic practice through a range of examples of the task and providing for a cumulative review of newly learned concepts.

Direct Instruction as a Cognitive Strategy

More recently, views of Direct Instruction have moved from the rather narrow definition of tightly sequenced instruction with constant feedback to views which emphasize the development of cognitive strategies. Key elements of this approach are the provision by the teacher of explicit strategy or skills instruction – explanations regarding *what* the strategy is and *when*, *where*, and *how* to use it, as well as *why* it should be used – and the gradual transfer of responsibility for learning from the teacher to the student (Martin, 2016). The focus in this approach is on solving problems and constructing meanings, so it differs somewhat from the 'lock-step' approach implied above. In short, while appearing teacher-centered, the emphasis is on the student's needs and responses, with the teacher awareness of student understanding being a priority.

In order to apply this approach effectively you should consider the following steps:

- begin a lesson with a short review of previous learning and a short statement of goals;
- present new material in small steps, providing for student practice after each step;
- give clear and detailed instructions and explanations;
- provide a high level of practice for all students;
- ask a large number of questions, check for student understanding, and obtain responses from all students;
- guide students during initial learning phases;
- provide systematic feedback and corrections; and
- provide explicit instruction and practice for seatwork exercises and, where necessary, monitor students during seatwork.

Direct or Indirect Teaching?

Different teaching strategies are effective for different learning situations and different students. The material to be taught is one primary consideration. Let's take a look at those teaching behaviors that research has shown to be most effective for teaching basic skills or factual material. These teaching behaviors that are effective for basic skills instruction have been organized into a model of *Explicit Teaching*, one application of Direct Instruction.

The following suggestions are based on this model, and you should find that they enhance students' motivation for learning too.

- Start each lesson by correcting the previous night's homework and reviewing what students have recently been taught.
- Tell your students the goals of the day's lesson. Present new information a little at a time, modeling procedures, giving clear examples, and checking often to make sure students understand.
- Give opportunities for guided practice; ask questions that give students opportunities to correctly repeat or explain the procedure or concept that has just been taught. Student participation should be active until all students are able to respond correctly.
- During guided practice, give students effective feedback. When students answer incorrectly, reteach the lesson if necessary. When students answer correctly, explain why the answer was right.
- When appropriate, allow students to practice using the new information independently. Assist when necessary, and permit student interaction and mutual help.
- At the end of each week, review the previous week's lessons and at the end of the month review what students have learned during the last four weeks. These reviews are important to consolidate information and memory.

What do these approaches to Direct Instruction have in common? One common element is that students experience a high level of success after each step of the learning activity during both guided and independent practice. The amount of the material presented, the extent of teacher-guided practice, and the length of time spent on independent practice should be determined by the age of the students and their previous knowledge of the content. Other features in common are presenting new material in small steps, modeling learning and guided practice, 'think alouds' by teachers and students, regulating the level of difficulty in the task, cueing learning, providing systematic corrections and feedback, supporting student corrections, and providing for independent practice.

Remember that these are the teaching functions that have been found to be most effective. However, they do not have to be followed as a series of prescribed steps: feedback to students, correction of errors and misunderstanding, and re-teaching must occur as necessary.

For unstructured material where skills do not have to be sequenced, or where there is no general rule to be learned and applied, such as in problem-solving activities, writing essays, analyzing literature, or creative expression, explicit teaching is obviously less appropriate and less effective. For this type of material, indirect approaches such as brainstorming, guided questioning, and cooperative group work are more appropriate.

A review of Liem and Martin (2020) shows that Direct Instruction is a very effective instructional technique in improving student performance. What might the reasons for the success of Direct Instruction be and how does it seem to facilitate student motivation? Three factors are decisive as reasons for its success. First, the teacher's classroom management is structured, leading to a very low rate of student interruptive behaviors. Second, the teacher maintains a strong academic focus and uses available instructional time intensively to initiate and facilitate students' learning activities. Last, the teacher ensures that as many students as possible achieve good learning progress by carefully choosing appropriate tasks, clearly presenting subject-matter information and solution strategies, continuously diagnosing each student's learning progress and learning difficulties, and providing effective help through remedial instruction.

QUESTION POINTS

?	What do you think of teacher attention as reinforcement? What are possible reasons that teachers find it difficult to use and what are the mistakes that teachers often make in its use?
?	Are there any problems in the use of extrinsic reinforcement? The use of extrinsic reinforcers at school (and we might add at home) is very widespread, although, often, very poorly used from a theoretical point of view. What is your thought on what was said by Walters and Grusec (1977, p. 124): *we have good reason to suspect that agents of socialization may well have diminished the effectiveness of social and material reinforcement by being too prodigal in its use, or at least by often administering it independent of the behavior engaged in.*
?	What do you think of the use of Direction Instruction and its underlying principles during the COVID-19 pandemic? Would this instructional method be effective in motivating and engaging students to learn at home (i.e., home-based learning) via *Zoom*?

ACTION STATIONS

- Students benefit from positive reinforcement. Consider exciting, innovative, and fun ideas for rewarding individuals or the entire class. Draft a pamphlet that presents your ideas on the use of creative reinforcement.
- Make a list of potential motivators that seem appropriate for primary school students, high school students, and young adults. List both tangible and non-tangible rewards and motivators. Some people find it easier to generate reinforcers for certain ages than others. Which group is the most difficult? Why?
- Revisit your personal case study and describe your new insights and solutions after reading this chapter.

REFERENCES AND RECOMMENDED READINGS

Adams, G., & Engelmann, S. (1996). *Research on direct instruction: 25 years beyond DISTAR*. Seattle, WA: Educational Achievement Systems.

Chua, A. (2011). *Battle hymn of the tiger mother*. New York, NY: Penguin Random House.

Ciaccio, J. (2004). *Totally positive teaching: A five-stage approach to energizing students and teachers*. Alexandria: Association for Supervision and Curriculum Development.

Datchuk, S. (2017). A direct instruction and precision teaching intervention to improve the sentence construction of middle school students with writing difficulties. *The Journal of Special Education*, *51*, 62–71.

Hattie, J., & Anderman, E. (Eds.). (2020). *International guide to student achievement* (2nd ed.). Oxford: Routledge.

Liem, G. A. D., & Martin, A. J. (2020). Direct instruction. In J. Hattie & E. Anderman (Eds.), *International guide to student achievement* (2nd ed., pp. 277–284). Oxford: Routledge.

Martin, A. J. (2016). *Using Load Reduction Instruction (LRI) to boost motivation and engagement*. Leicester: British Psychological Society.

Martin, A. J., & Evans, P. (2018). Load reduction instruction: Exploring a framework that assesses explicit instruction through to independent learning. *Teaching and Teacher Education 73*, 203–214.

Merret, F., & Wheldall, K. (1990). *Positive teaching in the primary school: Effective classroom behavior management*. London: Paul Chapman.

National Institute of Direct Instruction (NIFDI). (2017). *Writings on Direct Instruction: A bibliography*. Eugene, Oregon: Author. Retrieved from https://www.nifdi.org/docman/research/bibliography/205-di-bibliography-reference-list/file

Skinner, B. F. (1971). *Beyond freedom and dignity*. New York, NY: Alfred A. Knopf.

Skinner, B. F. (1977). The free and happy student. In H. F. Clarizio, R. C. Craig, & W. A. Mehrens (Eds.), *Contemporary issues in educational psychology*. Boston, MA: Allyn & Bacon.

Skinner, B. F. (1986). Programmed instruction revisited. *Phi Delta Kappan*, *68*, 103–110.

Walters, G. C., & Grusec, J. E. (1977). *Punishment*. San Francisco, CA: W. H. Freeman.

Weiner, B. (1990). History of motivational research in education. *Journal of Educational Psychology*, 82, 616–622.

Wheldall, K., & Merret, F. (1984/2019). *Positive teaching: The behavioral approach*. London: Allen & Unwin/New York, NY: Routledge.

Wheldall, K., & Merret, F. (1989). *Positive teaching in the secondary school: Effective classroom behavior management*. London: Paul Chapman.

7   SHOOTING FOR GOALS

'I'm no good at it at all,' griped Ben. 'I only came fourth and I really thought I should have beaten the others! I can't be bothered now!'

'Well, I enjoyed it anyhow,' replied Jenny. 'I don't care if I beat anyone else or not – you should really just worry about yourself.'

'It's all right for you to say that, but you don't have a mum and dad on your back all the time to be the best,' retorted the disgruntled Ben.

'That's true, but I do like to please them, and it's important to me that they think I try hard,' Ben added.

We have all seen individuals invest tremendous effort, great patience in learning, or perfecting particular behavior. No doubt you have seen boys and girls on the basketball court shooting for goals to improve their skills. Time and

DOI: 10.4324/9781003198383-8

time again they return to practice. Yet, often these same individuals appear bored in classrooms and bring very little effort to the academic tasks at hand. Conversely, many individuals are very involved in their classroom activities but feign sickness when sporting activities are on. You have seen these people listlessly sitting by the edge of the pool or lagging behind so that they are not chosen for a group sport.

HAVE YOU ENCOUNTERED SIMILAR CHALLENGES?

Describe a similar situation based on your observation of your students below.

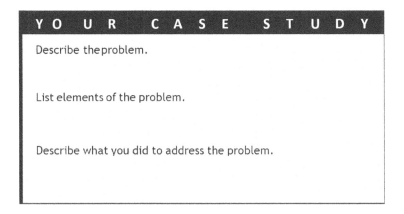

YOUR CASE STUDY

Describe the problem.

List elements of the problem.

Describe what you did to address the problem.

WHAT MIGHT BE THE PROBLEM?

What makes the difference in the investment of energy that some people bring to particular activities, but not others? In a sense, it is the goals for which we choose to invest our time and energy that make the difference. Goals that are important and achievable motivate us. At times we are very aware of these goals and consciously set out to achieve them. At other times we may have only a vague inkling of the goals that motivate us.

As we discussed in Chapter 5 (*I Believe I Can Do It*), there are two types of goal. First, there are goals for desired outcomes of the activity. These goals may be short-term, long-term, or sometimes a combination of the two. For example, a goal may be to complete an assignment, to become a good swimmer, or to save money to go on a holiday. These *outcome-focused* goals are very important as they give focus to the activities we do and often energize us to keep at tasks (e.g., relentless training) long after immediate interest flags. There are also goals related to the *how* of accomplishing outcome goals. These *process-focused* goals are as important as outcome-focused goals because they provide the clarity on how one should go about pursuing outcome goals and the direction toward attaining them. To complete an essay assignment, for example, the process-oriented goals entail understanding the task, breaking it into parts, searching for information on the Internet and at the library, taking notes on the reading materials, organizing information, writing a first draft of the essay, and so on. In other words, outcome goals represent our destination, whereas process goals represent the ways in which we can reach our destination.

But goals can also provide a framework for action and a lens through which individuals define success. These goals are called *goal orientations.* While there are various contents of the goals that may orient individual behavior (see Ford & Smith, 2020), those particularly pertinent to student learning motivation can be grouped in three broad categories: *mastery goals, performance goals,* and *social goals.* When the driving force behind an individual's involvement in an activity is its inherent interest or challenge, the excitement of discovery, the buzz from doing it well or the prospect of self-improvement, a mastery goal orientation is probably operating. Mastery motivation is very powerful and appears to be innate in us (recall what we discussed in Chapter 2 that, according to Self-Determination Theory, one of our basic psychological needs is the *need for competence*). When we are motivated by mastery, we often make an extra effort, seek a challenge just for the sake of it, take on extra work, and become very involved in what we are doing.

When the driving force behind an individual's involvement in an activity is the desire to compete, outdo other people, and be rewarded, a performance goal orientation is probably operating. In this case, the reference point for successful achievement is the relative performance of others. When we are motivated by performance goals, we are often very concerned about external assessment. The value of the activity is measured in terms of our relative success in achieving standards better than those attained by other people.

When the driving force behind our engagement in an activity is a desire to please our parents, teachers, or friends, to be important in the peer group, or to preserve our cultural identity, then a social goal orientation is probably operating. In this case, being successful means fulfilling social needs which might include being responsible, gaining approval, being liked, or being part of a group.

In addition to these goal orientations, individuals can also have *morality-based goals.* They arise within a motivational system in which the goal is to help others cooperatively in a group-work situation in the hope of increasing the group's achievement and overall welfare.

These goals are not mutually exclusive. In a particular activity, an individual may be motivated by all four at once! And each of these goals affects everyone at some time or another. The relative importance of one or other goal orientations at a particular time helps explain the motivation, or lack of it, which individuals bring to particular activities. Furthermore, outcome- and process-oriented goals are housed within these goal orientations. For example, an outcome goal might be to complete a history assignment. This goal may be achieved within a goal orientation framework with the following possible characteristics:

- *mastery* ('I want to do better on this assignment than I have done on previous assignments, and I will do this by doing in-depth research on the topic'), or
- *performance* ('I want to do better in this assignment than anyone else in the class, and I will ask for some cues to achieve this from Mrs. Jenkins'), or
- *social* ('I want to do better in this assignment to please my parents, and I will let them know how hard I work on it').

Of course, all might be operating at once. In getting to know the particular characteristics of the goal orientations that influence the motivation of individuals, knowledge of the reasons and aims that make one goal or other more important for the students at a particular time gives educators an important armory for changing and enhancing motivation.

What are the potential strengths and weaknesses of each of these goal orientations? Central to a mastery goal orientation is the belief that effort leads to success: the focus of attention is on the intrinsic value of learning. With a mastery goal, individuals are oriented toward developing new skills, trying to understand their work, improving their level of competence, or achieving a sense of 'mastery.' In other words, students feel successful if they believe they have personally improved, or have come to understand something. Their performance relative to others is irrelevant; it is the task and its mastery that are important. When the focus of attention is on effort, as is the case with mastery-oriented learning, pride and satisfaction are associated with successful effort, and guilt is associated with inadequate effort. As the relationship between ability and outcome is not an issue, the student is encouraged to expend greater effort to improve performance next time around. Mastery-oriented students are more likely to be more tolerant of failure and see it as a necessary condition for further effort in learning. It makes sense, therefore, that mastery-oriented students hold a growth mindset of ability. They believe that their skills and knowledge can be developed through effort and persistence (see Table 7.1).

In contrast, central to a performance goal orientation is a focus on one's ability relative to others and sense of self-worth (see Table 7.2). Ability is shown by doing better than others, by surpassing norms, or by achieving success with little effort. Public recognition for doing better than others is an important element of a performance goal orientation. Performance goals and achievements are referenced against the performance of others or against external standards such as marks or grades. Consequently, 'self-worth' is determined by one's achievement and perception of ability to perform relative to others. Hence, when an individual tries hard without being completely successful (in terms of the established norms), his or her sense of self-worth

Table 7.1 Characteristics of Mastery-oriented Students

Behavioral characteristics of mastery-oriented students

Students motivated by mastery goals:

- take extra effort in class even when there are no marks for it;
- seek challenging work for the sake of it;
- ask for additional work;
- ask more than the usual number of questions about their work; and
- make applications of school knowledge to the real world.

Affective characteristics of mastery-oriented students

Students motivated by mastery goals:

- are pleased when finding the solution to a problem;
- enjoy challenging work even though it is more difficult;
- are pleased when extra effort leads to a good result; and
- want to understand things even if it requires extra effort or explanation from the teacher.

Cognitive characteristics of mastery-oriented students

Students motivated by mastery goals:

- view personal progress or self-improvement as a benchmark of success;
- adopt a growth mindset, believing that effort leads to skill development;
- see tasks or tests as challenges rather than threats;
- attribute their success to effort and effective learning strategies; and
- view failure as a need to put in extra effort and adopt more effective strategies.

Source: Based on Dowson & McInerney (2001, 2003).

may be threatened. An overemphasis on ability means that we cannot make mistakes: if we do, we are dumb. An overemphasis on performance may also encourage unhealthy competition in which only a small number of students can be successful. If only a few are successful, many are failures, a status which induces unsuccessful students to engage in self-worth oriented or failure-avoiding behavior such as we have discussed in Chapter 3 (*Why Should I Do It?*). An overemphasis on performance can call into question the value of effort, because although the effort is admirable, in the long term it is the ability that counts. If after much effort an individual is still relatively unsuccessful, the only conclusion is that they lack ability and hence, as we have said above, perceive themselves as less competent. It is not surprising that performance-oriented students tend to hold a fixed mindset of ability. They believe that one's ability is innate and something that cannot be developed further even with effort and hard work (i.e., 'You are either born smart or not').

Within widely differing learning environments, it appears that mastery-oriented individuals are more prepared to spend time on learning tasks and become engaged in learning at a deeper level than those who are motivated by a performance goal orientation. Performance-oriented individuals may use surface-level strategies such as rote memorization and rehearsal in order to demonstrate that they 'know' more than others. Furthermore, because performance is

Table 7.2 Characteristics of Performance-oriented Students

Behavioral characteristics of performance-oriented students

Students motivated by performance goals:

- ask questions often about the teacher's expectations related to assignments;
- ask questions about the structure of assignments, especially how many marks are awarded to each section;
- do work beyond the usual expectations to get more marks; and
- question the distribution of exam and assignment marks.

Affective characteristics of performance-oriented students

Students motivated by performance goals:

- get upset when their academic results are not as good as expected;
- are never satisfied with anything less than becoming the best;
- are constantly concerned about relative performance; and
- are prone to test anxiety.

Cognitive characteristics of performance-oriented students

Students motivated by performance goals:

- view outperforming others, or becoming the top scorer, as a benchmark of success;
- adopt a fixed mindset, believing that ability is inborn and relatively stable;
- see tasks or tests as threats rather than challenges;
- attribute their success to ability; and
- view failure as a result of a lack of ability.

Source: Based on Dowson & McInerney (2001, 2003).

often a result of normative grading system, not only do performance-oriented students engage in social comparison, they also avoid challenging tasks (particularly when students have a low estimation of their own ability) and withdraw from tasks after an initial failure (why continue if one lacks ability?).

As we have suggested above, recent theorizing and research suggest that performance and mastery goals are not opposite ends of the same continuum, and that individuals may hold both, varying in importance depending on the nature of the task, the school environment, and the broader social and educational context of the school. Furthermore, students may hold multiple goals such as a desire to please their parents and teachers, to be important in the peer group, or to preserve their cultural identity, each of which may impact upon their level of motivation for particular tasks in school settings. Indeed, these multiple goals interact, providing a complex framework of motivational determinants of action. A student from a minority group, for example, may feel strong conflicting pressures both to maintain cultural values which may not foster academic achievement, and to achieve in a school context. This conflict can be especially acute for girls in some cultures. Meanwhile, yet another pressure is operating – that of being accepted and liked by one's peers. This may further influence whether doing well at school is seen as appropriate or not.

Social goals also influence motivation in a wide range of activities (see Table 7.3). There is no doubt that the desire to please our parents and significant

Table 7.3 Characteristics of Socially-oriented Students

Behavioral characteristics of socially oriented students

Students motivated by social goals:

- ask about marks and grades on behalf of their parents;
- work hard at school to please parents;
- make opportunities to talk to teachers;
- work hard to please teachers;
- become involved in social activities such as fundraising;
- become involved in peer tutoring and buddy programs; and
- make other students aware of rules and conventions.

Socially oriented students may also engage in activities that annoy teachers:

- pass notes in class;
- stake out an area in the playground; and
- want to work only with particular people.

Affective characteristics of socially oriented students

Students motivated by social goals:

- like and interact with peers beyond the immediate school situation;
- are upset when friends are reprimanded;
- feel a sense of pressure and anxiety when dealing with performance tasks; and
- enjoy working with others in a group.

Source: Based on Dowson & McInerney (2001, 2003).

others is a major determinant of motivation across a wide range of academic and non-academic areas. Younger students and students from collectivist cultural backgrounds are likely to be motivated by social goals more strongly than older students and students from individualist cultural traditions.

It is often thought that social goals, such as being seen as part of the peer group, may not encourage engagement with academic activities. In fact, however, such motives may be very powerful in influencing us to learn particular skills that may be perceived as important to maintain these social connections. While social goals do not appear to be particularly strong influences on academic performance within the school environment, where social goal motivation has been encouraged, there have been positive academic results. Cooperation, for example, is often associated with effort, sharing ideas, and achievement. It has been argued that cooperation enhances students' self-worth by de-emphasizing ability differences and that, through this, students experience support for contributing to the group effort and have more opportunities for success. With morality-based motivation, individual effort is seen in terms of contribution to a group product and helping others, for example, in cooperative teamwork. The *intention* of group members to help or expend effort takes priority over their actual ability to do so, irrespective of group success or failure.

If we feel strong about our capacities in an area, performance and social goals may be influencing our motivation to participate in an adaptive way.

On the other hand, if we lack confidence in an area, performance and social goals are likely to have a negative impact on our motivation to participate – who wants to be compared with others and potentially embarrassed in front of peers, friends, and family? In this latter case, the only effective goal with motivational potential is task or mastery orientation. In this case, perceived capacity is less threatening, as the hallmark of learning is personal (i.e., individual progress). Furthermore, interest in the task becomes the focus and, thus, allowing some joy in the learning task to emerge.

THINGS TO TRY

Despite the fact that both folklore and research support the major importance of mastery goals to learning, schools and other learning environments seem to emphasize performance goals relatively more strongly, at least when it counts at assessment time. When assessment is based on a norm-referenced grading system (i.e., the 'bell-curve' grading), there are only a handful of students who do well, many perform on an average level, and some perform below average. Grading becomes a zero-sum game exercise. Setting performance goal frameworks in classrooms, whether intentionally or inadvertently, circumscribes students' opportunities for experiencing success and, hence, is counterproductive to effective motivation.

How do you communicate achievement goals? There has been considerable research directed at examining ways in which various achievement goals are implicitly and explicitly communicated to learners. Achievement goals may be communicated to learners through the tasks that are set, the assessment and evaluation of behavior, the responsibility for the task set, and the monitoring of the level of achievement. How each of these aspects is designed determines the classroom and school goal structures. Some classrooms and schools emphasize mastery goals, whereas some others performance goals (see also Chapter 9 – *But I Teach Well, Don't I?*).

Clearly, the nature of the tasks set will influence whether learners are likely to become mastery-oriented or to strive for extrinsic goals such as grades and marks. Among key aspects of tasks that have been found to be related to mastery motivation are variety, diversity, challenge, control, and meaningfulness. When motivation is intrinsic, social comparison and other performance criteria become less important to the learner.

The way in which achievement is evaluated and recognized also influences the way in which the learner perceives the relevant goal. For example, if learning episodes are structured so that learners engage in intrinsically motivated learning and are then evaluated through non-competitive means, such as portfolios or comparisons with personal best, learners are likely to be mastery-oriented. Setting a clear rubric of assessment and making it available to students is also important in promoting students' adoption of a mastery goal orientation because students will be motivated to establish skills specified in the rubric rather than comparing their performance with those of others. On the other hand, if learning episodes are structured so that learners experience intrinsically motivated learning but are then evaluated through comparison with others, learners are likely to be performance-oriented. In this case, the 'real' goal of learning is understood by the learner as performance-based. Whenever evaluation is based upon social comparison, performance goals are established: the overt mastery goals established through the structure of the learning episodes are thereby undermined.

At some point, comparisons with others may be necessary, but these comparisons must be made in a way that does not diminish the value of the achievement for the individual. For example, many athletes come last in a race but are satisfied because they produced their personal best time. If the coach simply emphasized the fact that they came last, the athlete would have good reason to feel bad about their achievement, with the prospect of diminished motivation as a result. This athlete analogy can be aptly transferred to a school setting. Students should be encouraged to set personal best academic goals and pursue these to the best of their ability. We define personal best goals as the goals, outcome-oriented and process-oriented, that match, or are slightly more challenging than, the students' previous best attainment (Liem et al., 2012).

Another powerful factor that influences whether learners perceive learning as mastery-oriented or performance-oriented relates to who holds the power to make decisions about the tasks and their assessment. The extent to which learners perceive that they genuinely share authority and have significant levels of autonomy in making choices appears to be a significant factor in their engagement in learning and the quality of their effort. To the extent that external controls are reduced and learners have some meaningful level of control over the selection of tasks, materials, method of learning, product, pace, and assessment, they are more likely to be mastery-oriented than performance-oriented.

As we have suggested, many learning environments emphasize performance goals through competition and social comparison, ability grouping, and tracking, as well as public evaluation of performance and conduct based on normative standards of performance. In these environments, learners are given little opportunity to cooperate and interact with other learners, and little opportunity to choose the tasks that are of most interest and relevance to them. There are, of course, environments that emphasize mastery and social solidarity orientations. These environments give opportunities for peer interaction and cooperation; group students according to interest and needs; allow flexibility in choice of activities and opportunities for student initiative and responsibility; define success in terms of effort, progress, and improvement; and put an emphasis on the value and interest of learning. Learners in these settings are likely to be highly motivated, set themselves meaningful and challenging goals, and persist at learning for the perceived benefits that will accrue to them.

Helping Students Set Goals

In order to help students set outcome goals that are reasonable and motivational, within a framework of goal orientations that maximize this motivation, you need to get to know your students. Survey or interview students to find out about their unique needs, interests, and goals. Ascertain relevant information from parent–teacher interviews and consult demographic and school records. Observations of your students in the classroom and playground will also give you insights into their interests and needs. With this knowledge, you are in a position to provide individualized guidance about how a student's personal goals fit in with the learning goals established for the class. It also enables you to structure educational goals and activities to meet the needs of students.

It is also very useful to have goal-setting activities where you demonstrate the relationship between effort, achieving the goal, and 'payoff.' In particular, show students how to:

- define goals clearly;
- set personalized goals or personal best goals, such that students have a sense of ownership and stronger commitment to their goals;
- relate their interests and goals to learning content and learning activities;
- analyze goals to establish steps in their accomplishment;
- consider impediments and challenges to achieving goals;
- consider solutions to these impediments and challenges;
- set time limits for achieving targets;
- evaluate progress; and
- reward themselves for attainment of goals.

Personal Investment in Achieving Goals

Schooling does not consist solely of learning academic material. Indeed, the social dimension of schooling (including the influence of parents, teachers, and peers) may be equally important and extremely influential in affecting students' attitudes toward schooling in general and learning in particular. A goal model of motivation, which considers other relevant and interacting goals, has been used in a number of studies of student motivation. This approach is called the *Personal Investment* theory of motivation (King, Datu, & McInerney, 2018; Maehr & Braskamp, 1986). This model is helpful in conceptualizing motivation as it emphasizes that students may hold multiple goals, each of which may impact upon their level of motivation for particular tasks, and that there is a potential interaction between a variety of important goals for students in school-related areas.

In the Personal Investment Theory, goals are broadly classified as *task, ego, social solidarity,* and *extrinsic rewards.* Task goals emphasize the intrinsic interest of the learning exercise where the goal of learning is to gain understanding, insight, or skill. Learning in and of itself is valued, and the attainment of mastery is seen as dependent on one's effort. Ego and extrinsic goals emphasize individual comparison and competition, and achievement is seen as the means of obtaining external rewards. Social solidarity goals emphasize the cooperative and affiliative dimensions of learning specifically to enhance and preserve group solidarity. Among social goals that have been found influential in determining a student's motivation at school are approval, responsibility, welfare, affiliation, and survival.

Each of the goal categories described in the Personal Investment model impacts upon an individual's sense of competence, autonomy, and purpose in learning, and contributes to their motivational orientation. Our own research indicates that classrooms and schools should emphasize task and social solidarity goals. Unfortunately, many schools emphasize ego and extrinsic goals through competition and social comparison, ability grouping and tracking, public evaluation of performance, and conduct based on normative standards of performance. Such schools give students little opportunity to cooperate and interact with other students, and little opportunity to choose the tasks that are of most interest and relevance to them. There are, of course, classrooms and schools that emphasize task and social solidarity orientations. These classrooms give opportunities for peer interaction and cooperation; group students according to interest and needs rather than ability; provide opportunities for the student to make decisions; define success in terms of personal progress and self-improvement rather than competition and relative performance; and put an emphasis on the value of effort rather than achievement. Students in these classrooms are more likely to be motivated, dare to try by setting meaningful and challenging goals.

QUESTION POINTS

?	Competition is a powerful incentive since it brings the full force of group pressure to bear upon the learner. On the other hand, it can be dangerous and should be used judiciously. How might competition be used judiciously and effectively?
?	What are the potential effects on students of each of the following classroom procedures: (a) ability streaming; (b) mixed-ability classrooms; (c) mastery learning; (d) competition? In particular, discuss the effects on high-need and low-need achievers.
?	What is the importance of classroom goal structure in influencing motivation and relationships with others? Differentiate between, and give examples of, cooperative, competitive, and individualistic classroom goal structures.
?	Cooperation is what we teachers preach, but individual achievement and competition are what we practice. How can we be teaching the social skills and values of cooperation in learning when we continue to assess children's individual academic performance against others and grade them accordingly?

ACTION STATIONS

- How much classroom authority do you think your students would say you share with them? Consider situations such as choosing topics for study, deciding tasks for completion and assessment, and selecting methods of evaluation. In which areas do you share control with your students? How do you share control with them? What changes could you make to improve this?
- In this chapter, we have described achievement goal orientations (mastery, performance, and social goals) as students' psychological framework that gives meaning and purpose to their activities. Try to get to know the predominant goal orientations of your students. For example, can your students explain what is important to them? What are they trying to achieve? Can they relate this to their learning in the classroom? Do they predominantly work for performance, mastery, or social goals? Are they competitive? Do they prefer to work individually or in social groups? How important is family, teacher, and peer approval of their work? If they cannot explain the goals for their work and relate them to their learning in the classroom, they are unlikely to be very motivated.
- Use the information you gather in the previous action station to improve your classroom activities so that your students more adequately represent achievement goals that are important to them. Consider your classroom processes: which goal orientations seem to be emphasized? Do your emphases mesh with the emphases of the students? If they don't, there is likely to be a clash of values within your classroom which will inhibit effective motivation and learning.
- You might become aware during this exercise that some students are unable to express the goals for their work at school. You might find it useful to help these students clarify their personal goals and relate these to their learning goals.
- Design a classroom activity for teaching goal setting to your students.
- Revisit your personal case study and describe your new insights and solutions after reading this chapter.

REFERENCES AND RECOMMENDED READINGS

Bardach, L., Oczlon, S., Pietschnig, J., & Lüftenegger, M. (2020). Has achievement goal theory been right? A meta-analysis of the relation between goal structures and personal achievement goals. *Journal of Educational Psychology, 112*, 1197–1220.

Dowson, M., & McInerney, D. M. (2001). Psychological parameters of students' social and work avoidance goals: A qualitative investigation. *Journal of Educational Psychology, 93*, 35–42.

Dowson, M., & McInerney, D. M. (2003) What do students say about their motivational goals? Towards a more complex and dynamic perspective on student motivation. *Contemporary Educational Psychology, 28*, 91–113.

Elliot, A. J., & Hulleman, C. S. (2017). Achievement goals. In A. J. Elliot, C. S. Dweck, & D. S. Yeager (Eds.). *Handbook of competence and motivation: Theory and application* (pp. 43–60). New York, NY: The Guilford Press.

Elliot, A. J., Murayama, K., & Pekrun, R. (2011). A 3×2 achievement goal model. *Journal of Educational Psychology, 103*, 632–648.

Ford, M. E., & Smith, P. R. (2020). *Motivating self and others: Thriving with social purpose, life meaning, and the pursuit of core personal goals.* Cambridge: Cambridge University Press.

Hamamura, T., & Heine, S. J. (2008). Approach and avoidance motivation across cultures. In A. J. Elliot (Ed.). *Handbook of approach and avoidance motivation* (pp. 557–570). New York, NY: Psychology Press.

Huang, C. (2016). Achievement goals and self-efficacy: A meta-analysis. *Educational Research Review, 19*, 119–137.

King, R. B. (2017). Is a performance- avoidance achievement goal always maladaptive? Not necessarily for collectivists. *Personality and Individual Differences, 99*, 190–195.

King, R. B., Datu, J. A., & McInerney, D. M. (2018). Personal investment theory: A cross-cultural framework for the study of student motivation. In G. A. D. Liem, & D. M. McInerney (Eds.). *Big theories revisited 2* (pp. 69–88). Charlotte, NC: Information Age Publishing.

King, R. B., & McInerney, D. M. (2014). Culture's consequences on student motivation: Capturing cross-cultural universality and variability through personal investment theory. *Educational Psychologist, 49*, 175–198.

Liem, G. A. D. (2016). Academic and social achievement goals: Their additive, interactive, and specialized effects on school functioning. *British Journal of Educational Psychology, 86*, 37–56.

Liem, G. A. D., & Elliot, A. J. (2018). Sociocultural influences on achievement goal adoption and regulation: A goal complex perspective. In G. A. D. Liem, & D. M. McInerney (Eds.). *Big theories revisited 2* (pp. 41–67). Charlotte, NC: Information Age Publishing.

Liem, G. A. D., Ginns, P., Martin, A. J., Stone, B., & Herrett, M. (2012). Personal best goals and academic and social functioning: A longitudinal perspective. *Learning and Instruction, 22*, 222–230.

Liem, G. A. D., Lau, S., & Nie, Y. (2008). The role of self-efficacy, task value, and achievement goals in predicting learning strategies, task disengagement, peer relationship and English achievement outcome. *Contemporary Educational Psychology, 33*, 486–512.

Maehr, M. L., & Braskamp, L. A. (1986). *The motivation factor: A theory of personal investment.* Lexington: Health & Co.

Martin, A. J., & Elliot, A. J. (2016). The role of personal best (PB) goal setting in students' academic achievement gains. *Learning and Individual Differences, 45*, 222–227.

Scherrer, V., Preckel, F., Schmidt, I., & Elliot, A. J. (2020). Development of achievement goals and their relation to academic interest and achievement in adolescence: A review of the literature and two longitudinal studies. *Developmental Psychology, 56*, 795–814.

Senko, C. (2016). Achievement goal theory: A story of early promises, eventual discords, and future possibilities. In K. R. Wentzel, & D. B. Miele (Eds.). *Handbook of motivation at school* (pp. 75–95). New York, NY: Routledge.

Wentzel, K. (2018). A competence-in-context approach to understanding motivation at school. In G. A. D. Liem, & D. M. McInerney (Eds.). *Big theories revisited 2* (pp. 193–212). Charlotte, NC: Information Age Publishing.

Zusho, A., & Clayton, K. (2011). Culturalizing achievement goal theory and research. *Educational Psychologist, 46*, 239–260.

8 HOW DO I FEEL?

Adam often performs poorly on his Science tests. When he was sitting for the Science final examination, he felt very nervous and left many of the questions unanswered. Adam wore an anxious facial expression and was scared that he would fail the exam. At the same time, he could feel his heart pounding and he began to sweat profusely. All he wanted was to run away and not take the exam. Failing to concentrate, Adam was wondering, 'What would my two neighbors, Joanna and Emily, think of me if I fail?'

After the exam, Mrs. Stuart, Adam's Science teacher, asked, 'How did you prepare for the exam, Adam?' Adam replied, 'I started studying two days ago ..., trying to commit the chapters to my memory. To feel more relaxed, I watched my favorite TV programs and occasionally checked my mobile phone for messages.'

DOI: 10.4324/9781003198383-9

It is possible that a student who does well in many school subjects may feel uneasy when learning and taking a test in a particular subject. Educators call this test anxiety. Multiple reasons and factors – personal and contextual – may contribute to this unpleasant feeling. These include prior achievement, fear of failure, lack of perceived competence in the subject, lack of preparation for the test, and the nature of the examination. Test anxiety, however, is only one of the many different emotions that learners may experience. As we learn in this chapter, some of the emotions that students feel are pleasant whereas some others are unpleasant. Understanding students' emotions is particularly important as these emotions may affect their motivation, learning, and performance.

HAVE YOU ENCOUNTERED SIMILAR CHALLENGES?

Recall your teaching experience when a student in your class looked bored during your class or anxious during a test. Describe and unpack that situation below.

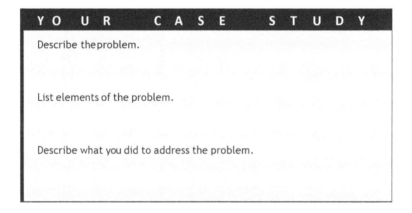

WHAT MIGHT BE THE PROBLEM?

Students, especially those in their adolescence, feel a variety of emotions in their schooling lives. These emotions are experienced when they are studying or in relation to their performance on a task or test. Some students find mathematics enjoyable, but some others find it boring. Even the same score on the same test, 65, may invoke different emotions in two different students, with one feeling proud for the hard work that he or she has put in, while the other feeling ashamed knowing that he or she could have put in more effort. Whether or not students realize what they feel about the score, these emotions may have an impact on their subsequent motivation to learn and the extent to which they put in effort in studying for the next test.

As part of a day-to-day schooling experience that has important implications for motivation, learning, and performance, student emotion has been an important and growing area of research in the past 20 years. In order to better understand the different emotions that students experience and their impacts on motivation, Reinhard Pekrun (2017, 2018, 2019) proposes an Achievement Emotion Theory. He views emotion as a multifaceted phenomenon that includes students' subjective feelings, cognitions, motivational propensities, physiological processes, and expressive/observable behavior. Based on this definition, let's consider Adam at the beginning of this chapter. Adam, who experienced a severe test anxiety, felt uneasy and nervous (*affective component*); worried about a possible failure and engaged in task–irrelevant thoughts by thinking of how Joanna and Emily would see him when he fails (*cognitive component*); wished he could flee from the test setting (*motivational component*); had a pounding heart and profuse sweat (*physiological component*); and showed an anxious face (*expressive component*). Before we can help students cope with their test anxiety and perform better, we first need to recognize these symptoms.

Achievement emotions, according to the Achievement Emotion model, differ along two dimensions: *valence* and *activation*. In terms of valence, *positive* or *pleasant* emotions can be distinguished from *negative* or *unpleasant* emotions. Enjoyment, hope, and gratitude are examples of positive emotions, whereas anxiety, boredom, and sadness are examples of negative emotions. In terms of activation, *physiologically activating* emotions such as pride or anger, can be contrasted with *physiologically deactivating* emotions like relief or hopelessness. As we can see from these examples, the valence and activation dimensions are mutually exclusive; this means there are four possible categories of achievement emotions: *positive activating, positive deactivating, negative activating,* and *negative deactivating* emotions. Students may experience each group of these emotions in relation to the object that they focus on: *learning activities* (i.e., *during studying*) or *outcomes* (i.e., *past* or *future*). Table 8.1 shows the classification of achievement emotions and their examples as Pekrun proposes.

The theory further suggests that positive activating emotions (e.g., enjoyment, joy, gratitude, and hope) may strengthen student motivation to learn, whereas positive deactivating emotions (e.g., relaxation, contentment, relief, and pride) may decrease immediate motivation but increase long-term motivation. As for negative activating emotions (e.g., anger, anxiety, and shame), they may lower intrinsic motivation but may foster extrinsic motivation to study harder (in order not to fail). Lastly, negative deactivating emotions (i.e., boredom, sadness, disappointment, and hopelessness) decrease student motivation.

Aligned with Social-Cognitive Theory, Pekrun believes that the types of emotions that students feel depend on their perceptions or appraisals of two aspects of achievement activities: the perceived *control* over the tasks and their outcomes (success *vs.* failure) and the perceived *value* (or *importance*) of

Table 8.1 Classification of Achievement Emotions

Object Focus	Valence	Activation	Emotion	What Might Students Say?
Present Learning Activities	Positive	Activating	Enjoyment	*I really like learning about this topic. Things do make sense to me!*
		Deactivating	Relaxation	*I will take it easy… I have nothing to lose for this homework.*
	Negative	Activating	Anger	*Why do I have to learn all these? I am not interested at all.*
		Deactivating	Frustration	*I have tried hard understanding this material, but I still can't make sense of it.*
		Deactivating	Boredom	*This is too easy for me. I have gone through this several times before.*
Future Outcomes	Positive	Activating	Hope	*I have done my best studying for the test. I believe I will do well on it.*
		Deactivating	Anticipatory Joy	*I will be delighted if I could get an A for the upcoming test.*
		Deactivating	Anticipatory Relief	*Thank God…, I finally understand these materials. I will do well tomorrow.*
	Negative	Activating	(Test) Anxiety	*I am afraid I may fail on this important exam.*
		Deactivating	Hopelessness	*I don't think I will pass the quiz tomorrow. I won't bother trying.*
Past Outcomes	Positive	Activating	Joy	*Hooray, I got a perfect score!*
		Activating	Pride	*I didn't give up even when I initially couldn't understand the formulas. Glad that I tried and my hard work paid off!*
		Deactivating	Gratitude	*I am thankful to Mrs. Stuart for taking the extra time to explain the materials to me.*
		Deactivating	Contentment	*Receiving 60 out of 100 was more that I could expect.*
		Deactivating	Relief	*I thought I would fail on the test, but I passed!*
	Negative	Activating	Shame	*I knew I should have studied for the test instead of playing basketball.*
		Activating	Anger	*The exam was just outrageously difficult. None of the materials I learned were tested. Nobody could do it!*
		Deactivating	Sadness	*Sigh… I failed again.*
		Deactivating	Disappointment	*I thought I would do well on the exam…, but I did not.*

Source: Adapted from Harley et al. (2019).

those tasks and their outcomes (success *vs.* failure). This is the reason why the theory is called the Control-Value Model of Achievement Emotion. More specifically, the combination of students' perceptions of control and value generate different achievement emotions. Enjoyment in studying, for example, may be a result of having positive perceptions of ability in mastering the learning material (i.e., high control) and seeing the importance of the learning material (i.e., high value). In contrast, feeling anxious about the upcoming examination may be a consequence of seeing the test or the subject as important while at the same time having low perceived competence in mastering the learning material (i.e., low control). The degree to which students' positive emotions depend on their perceived competence and values, instructional strategies and practices relevant to strengthening these two subjective beliefs, as we discussed in Chapter 3 (*Why Should I Do It?*) and Chapter 5 (*I Believe I Can Do It*), are also applicable to foster students' positive emotions.

Students may also experience mixed emotions triggered by specific, new situations they are in, or specific, non-routine tasks they are assigned to do. These emotions, for example, may include surprise and confusion about a new task, or curiosity and at the same time frustration about the conflicting information presented to them. Students' emotions may also be aroused because of a specific topic presented in lessons or learning materials. I (Gregory) recall my experience when an adult student, who was in her early twenties, expressed her sadness and cried while watching a movie together in the class. Upon my conversation with the student, I found out that the storyline of the movie reminded her of the recent passing of her loved one. Compassion, love, empathy, sympathy, admiration, contempt, envy, and anger are, therefore, among the social emotions that students may experience when tasked to read a novel or watch a movie. Indeed, using songs and movies to promote development of students' awareness of their emotions and of their social awareness is a common practice in social and emotional learning programs (see Durlak et al., 2015 and www.casel.org).

Anxiety and School Motivation

Relative to other achievement emotions, anxiety is the achievement emotion that has been more widely researched in educational settings, especially considering its debilitating effects on performance. Many students experience moderate to severe anxiety within the school setting that inhibits motivation and effective learning. Such anxiety can be general (i.e., an overall feeling of unease while at school), or it can be more specifically related to particular subjects, teachers, or school practices (e.g., testing and evaluation). It appears that general forms of anxiety increase as students move from primary into secondary grades. This has been associated with changing school environments. Secondary schools are more evaluative and competitive, and social comparisons become more prevalent. Other factors that are thought to increase school anxiety are moving from a smaller to a larger school, having different teachers (and classmates) throughout the school day, experiencing ability grouping, and having fewer opportunities for decision making and less autonomy. One specific form of anxiety is test anxiety (Zeidner, 1998, 2014, 2020).

What is test anxiety? Does it affect all students? How does test anxiety affect motivation and learning, and what can the teacher do to prevent or minimize any of its negative effects? Let us consider the issues now.

Research in the area of anxiety has differentiated between individuals who show *state anxiety*, which is experienced only in certain situations such as exams or learning to use a computer, and those for whom anxiety is a *trait* which generally affects much of what they do in their lives. Test anxiety is an example of the former. Specifically, it is a state of anxiety about not performing well when being evaluated in a test situation. The anxiety is experienced by those for whom the test situation involves a perceived threat to self-esteem such as self-worth-oriented and learned-helpless students that we discussed in Chapter 3 (*Why Should I Do It?*). However, students who are ill-prepared for the test and don't understand their work as well as students who lack effective study skills are likely to suffer from test anxiety too.

According to Irwin Sarason and Barbara Sarason (1990), test anxiety has cognitive and emotional/physical components. Cognitively, test-anxious students tend to engage in task-irrelevant thoughts (e.g., self-preoccupation, failure-centeredness, helplessness, escapism, and thoughts concerning what other people think) and worry (e.g., troubled about the nature of the task, fret about doing badly, inability to focus on the task, and bothered about how others perform). Emotionally, test-anxious students feel jittery, nervous, distressed, uneasy, short-tempered, and moody. They are unable to relax. Physically, it is likely that test-anxious students suffer from the following psychosomatic symptoms prior to the test: a headache, a stomach cramp (i.e., butterflies in the stomach), palpitations, sweaty palms, a loss of appetite, and nausea.

International studies on test anxiety have shown that students in certain cultures are more prone to suffer from test anxiety than those in other cultures (OECD, 2017). It is very likely that these students' test anxiety is rooted in their fear of failure (OECD, 2019) which may grow out of the perceived importance of academic success and the social pressure of performing well from parents, teachers, and even the society. Fear of failure aside, why are some students more test anxious than others? There are various reasons or causes underlying test anxiety. Let us have a closer look at these now.

One of the reasons suggests that some test-anxious students find it hard to focus attention on the task at hand because of self-doubt and thoughts generated in the evaluative situation that are irrelevant to the task (e.g., worrying about how one is doing rather than concentrating on the task at hand). It is believed that these thoughts interfere with the retrieval of learned material and that students perform poorly as a consequence. A deep breathing exercise that helps students calm prior to the test may be effective in reducing the anxiety of these students.

Another possible reason points to the ineffective information-processing skills (or cognitive strategies) of some highly test-anxious students as the main factor in their anxiety and poor academic performance in test situations. This means that, for highly test-anxious students with poor study habits, a training program that targets their study skills is likely to do well in reducing their anxiety and improving their performance in a test situation. We will discuss this in greater detail below.

THINGS TO TRY

The emotions that students experience when studying, or in relation to their past or anticipated outcomes, are their natural responses to the achievement situation. However, negative emotions can have debilitating impacts on student motivation, learning, and overall performance. Research has shown how negative emotions are associated with poorer attention, memory, decision making, creativity, mental and physical well-being, as well as lower capacity to build and maintain positive relationships (Pekrun, 2017). In contrast, as posited by the Broaden-and-Build Theory (Fredrickson, 2001), positive emotions help individuals *broaden* their awareness and perspectives and enable them to see the 'big picture' of a situation, and at the same time help individuals *build* resources and coping skills and make them more resilient.

Promoting Emotion Regulatory Skills

Educators may help students deal with their emotions effectively by fostering their emotion regulatory skills. Emotion regulation refers to the process by which individuals monitor and take control of the type, intensity, and duration of emotion they experience, realize the factors or reasons that trigger their emotion, and know how to express their emotion in a socially acceptable way. In the context of academic work, emotion regulation refers to students being able to identify their experienced emotions, change their emotions when they hinder students' goal pursuit, and harness their emotions as energy or source of motivation (Harley et al., 2019).

A variety or ways, strategies, and approaches to promoting students' emotion regulatory skills have now been developed. One of the most widely validated approaches is the RULER approach (see https://www.rulerapproach. org) designed by the Yale Center of Emotional Intelligence, founded and directed by Marc Brackett (https://www.marcbrackett.com). The RULER approach to emotion regulation encourages us to teach students the following steps:

- **R**ecognizing emotions in self and others;
- **U**nderstanding the causes and consequences of emotions;
- **L**abelling emotions accurately with a nuanced vocabulary;
- **E**xpressing emotions appropriately according to social norms and cultural contexts; and
- **R**egulating emotions effectively with helpful strategies.

Brackett (2019) says that an ability to label our emotion is key. If we can name the emotion we feel, we can 'tame' it. However, while recognizing and labeling emotions accurately may be something natural for many adults (but, you may be surprised!), this may not be the case for children and adolescents. Recall the different discreet achievement emotions shown in Table 8.1 You can use this list of emotions for a class discussion with your students. Ask them to identify the situations in which a student feels or experiences specific emotions (e.g., enjoyment, anger, frustration, gratitude). What are the factors that may trigger these emotions? Would these emotions be manifested and expressed in different ways in different cultural contexts? What can students do to change a negative emotion to a positive one and use the latter as a source of their motivation to learn?

Are There Effective Means of Alleviating Test Anxiety?

Let us now focus on test anxiety. What are the effective strategies to reduce it? The strategies depend on factors underlying students' test anxiety. When students are test anxious because they find it hard to focus on the task at hand and engage in thoughts irrelevant to the task (e.g., worrying about how one is doing rather than concentrating on the task), the most effective treatment may be a program which desensitizes the students to the anxiety-producing elements of the exam situation so that attention can be focused on the task itself. For these students, strategies that teach them how to deal with their interfering thoughts can be most effective. In particular, training in relaxation techniques (e.g., deep breathing exercise) paired with visualization of anxiety-producing test situations (e.g., entering the exam room, seeing printed exam questions, and receiving grades) can be beneficial.

When students are test anxious because of their ineffective information-processing or cognitive strategies, it is important to improve the student's study habits and metacognitive skills. Training in the PQ4R technique that has students preview, question, read, reflect, recite, and review material, for example, can improve performance in situations perceived as evaluative, because knowledge of material is increased and anxiety is decreased because of greater metacognitive awareness of improved mastery in these students (see also 'direct instruction' in Chapter 6).

An individual's perceived self-efficacy in coping with situations can also regulate anxiety arousal. The stronger an individual's belief that they can cope, the bolder they are in taking on threatening situations. Students who have a low sense of their own efficacy in managing academic demands are especially vulnerable to test anxiety. Perhaps one of the best ways of alleviating this is to develop = students' cognitive capabilities and self-regulatory skills for managing academic task demands and debilitating thoughts (see Chapter 5 – *I Believe I Can Do It*)

There will always be a number of students in your care who are anxious about evaluation. It is important that you identify and address the source of their anxiety before motivation to achieve becomes seriously affected. Knowing that for high test-anxious students, grading and testing may reduce their performance or even seriously debilitate them, you need to consider the matter of assessment carefully.

Effective reduction of anxiety involves the use of coping strategies to remove or circumvent the cause of stress and to deal with the reactions and emotions that are experienced. Students may use the following coping strategies (Zeidner, 1995, p. 124):

> *problem-focused* coping which tries to manage or solve the problem by dealing with the source of the stress in a positive way, e.g., through planning, collecting resources, studying hard; *emotion-focused* coping which tries to reduce the emotional symptoms associated with stress, e.g., talking to friends to gain reassurance, crying, denying the importance of the situation; *avoidance-oriented coping* which tries to avoid the stressful situation, e.g., isolating oneself from others, wasting time on irrelevant tasks, watching television excessively.

It is clear that, while emotion-focused or avoidance-oriented coping might help the individual keep an emotional balance for a short time, they may become maladaptive or even dysfunctional over time. There are plenty of examples of the negative long-term effects of ventilation of emotions, mental disengagement, binge eating and the use of tension-relieving substances such as alcohol and drugs, where the maladaptive nature of such coping strategies becomes evident.

Students should be encouraged and taught how to use problem-focused coping strategies. In relation to important tests or exams, the stressor cannot be removed. However, reducing the perceived threat that it poses can be achieved by planning a study schedule, increasing study time, and working with a friend or parent on revising important material. Such coping strategies are adaptive in that they are problem-focused and provide a sense of mastery over the stressor. This sense of personal control over the situation changes the perspective, diverting attention into a positive direction. It also helps to reduce the physiological and emotional reactions that initially build up at the anticipatory stage: 'What am I going to do to cope? There are all these demands on me.'

One method of helping students for whom the test situation is debilitating is to reduce the perceived threat of evaluation. Covington and Omelich (1987), for example, provided opportunities for students to re-sit an exam with unlimited time in which to complete answers. They found that for students who were well prepared, this opportunity inhibited anxiety and allowed original learning to be effectively retrieved. Not surprisingly, for those who were poorly prepared (although anxious) the inhibition of anxiety did not improve performance.

As discussed in Chapter 3 (*Why Should I Do It?*), researchers distinguish between failure-avoiding and failure accepting students. Students who are failure-avoiding (highly anxious, with good study skills) are motivated to achieve in order to maintain their sense of personal value which is judged by external performance. However, they are anxious that, if they fail despite all of their efforts, they will be seen as lacking in ability. On the other hand, students who fail repeatedly because of poor study skills will be anxious but failure-accepting, believing that their failure is an indication of low ability. Over time, such students will become resigned to defeat, having little or no motivation to achieve, a situation akin to learned helplessness.

In order to alleviate the effects of anxiety in the classroom, therefore, you could implement the following strategies:

- teach effective study habits to students and periodically review them;
- train students to be test-wise (e.g., teach test-taking strategies);
- teach relaxation techniques such as deep breathing exercises;
- utilize desensitization strategies such as exposure to 'mock' exam situations (or habituation), as appropriate;
- ensure that auditory and visual distracters are absent from test environment;
- reduce time pressures in evaluative situations;
- de-emphasize the evaluative nature of the task in test situations;
- emphasize the nature of the task and self-evaluation relative to previous performance rather than competition and student–student comparison;
- whenever possible, give students detailed feedback on their performance that is task-related and shows them how to improve (e.g., qualitative comments) rather than ego-related (e.g., grades and praise). In this way, intrinsic motivation will be fostered and concerns about self-worth will be minimized;
- provide opportunities for over-striving (well-prepared) anxious students to meet as a group with the teacher to share concerns. Often this reassurance will reduce anxiety considerably;
- provide models of anxious individuals engaging in successful task- completion strategies;
- provide more organized instructional material for highly anxious students;

- arrange test items in order of difficulty level, starting with least difficult and ending with most; and
- ensure that test items are of appropriate level of difficulty because anxiety increases with perceived task difficulty.

Students should be taught to recognize signs of anxiety such as negative talk about themselves ('I can't do this'; 'I'm going to fail'), fearfulness, irritability, avoidance and worry, and to practice positive self-talk ('I can do this if I try/ ask for more help/work harder/manage my time better/don't allow myself to be distracted'). Coaching students to re-appraise, re-frame, or re-interpret achievement events or situations is also helpful in alleviating anxiety. At the end of the day, people have little control over what happens to them, but they have control over how they view the world and react to difficulties. How people think affect how they feel and what they do! Indeed, this is the essence of the Cognitive-Behavioral Therapy or CBT.

Students should also learn and use relaxation techniques: deep breathing, muscle contraction and relaxation, brisk exercise, conscious 'emptying' of mind and focusing on a positive image. Anxious students should be encouraged to talk to others who tend to be anxious and to share their worries. They should also be encouraged to talk to and confide in significant adults (e.g., parents or other family members) about their concerns and be prepared to listen to others' advice.

It is also very beneficial for anxious students to set short-term achievable goals rather than global, long-term goals and to practice working to a time limit for some tasks. Confidence is built up when students begin to be successful. One way to increase feelings of success is for students to learn study skills (e.g., from teachers, friends, books) and reward themselves with special privileges when they practice them successfully.

QUESTION POINTS

?	Which appraisal do you believe is more important in generating your students' achievement emotions: their perceived control over a learning task or perceived value of the task? Consider specific achievement emotion in your answers.
?	How do you think students' achievement emotions impact their motivation to learn, level of engagement and, in turn, quality of their performance? Consider concrete examples in your answers.
?	We have little control over what happens to us, but we have control over how we view the world and respond to challenges. How do you interpret this statement from the Control-Value Theory of Achievement Emotion?

ACTION STATIONS

- Reflect on your own motivation in teaching. To what extent is it affected by the emotions you experience? How adequate is the Control-Value Model of Achievement Emotions as an explanation of your personal motivation in teaching?
- Based on the RULER approach, develop a plan that you could use with your students to foster their emotion regulatory skills. Implement and monitor the plan. Target specific students and observe its effect on them.
- Revisit your personal case study and describe your new insights and solutions after reading this chapter.

REFERENCES AND RECOMMENDED READINGS

Brackett, M. (2019). *Permission to feel: The unlocking the power of emotions to help our kids, ourselves, and our society thrive.* New York, NY: Celadon Books.

Camacho-Morles, J., Slemp, G. R., Pekrun, R., Loderer, K., Hou, H., & Oades, L. G. (2021). Activity achievement emotions and academic performance: A meta-analysis. *Educational Psychology Review.* Advance online publication.

Covington, M. V., & Omelich, C. L. (1987). I knew it cold before the exam: A test of the anxiety-blockage hypothesis. *Journal of Educational Psychology, 79,* 393–400.

Durlak, J. A., Domitrovich, C. E., Weissberg, R. P., & Gullotta, T. (Eds.). (2015). *Handbook of social and emotional learning: Research and practice.* New York, NY: Guilford.

Fredrickson, B. L. (2001). The role of positive emotions in positive psychology: The broaden-and-build theory of positive emotions. *American Psychologist, 56,* 218–226.

Harley, J. M., Pekrun, R., Taxer, J. L., & Gross, J. J. (2019). Emotion regulation in achievement situations: An integrated model. *Educational Psychologist, 54,* 106–126.

Pekrun, R. (2017). Emotion and achievement during adolescence. *Child Development Perspectives, 11,* 215–221.

Pekrun, R. (2018). Control-value theory: A social-cognitive approach to achievement emotions. In G. A. D. Liem, & D. M. McInerney (Eds.). *Big theories revisited 2* (pp. 162–190). Charlotte, NC: Information Age Publishing.

Pekrun, R. (2019). Achievement emotions: A control-value theory. In R. Patulny, A. Bellocchi, R. E. Olson, S. Khorana, J. McKenzie, & M. Peterie (Eds.). *Emotions in late modernity* (pp. 142–157). New York, NY: Routledge.

Pekrun, R., Lichtenfeld, S., Marsh, H. W., Murayama, K., & Goetz, T. (2017). Achievement emotions and academic performance: Longitudinal models of reciprocal effects. *Child Development, 88,* 1653–1670.

Pekrun, R., & Linnenbrink-Garcia, E. (2012). Academic emotions and student engagement. In S. Christenson, A. Reschly, & C. Wylie (Eds.). *Handbook of research on student engagement* (pp. 259–282). Boston, MA: Springer.

Pekrun, R., & Linnenbrink-Garcia, L. (2014). *International handbook of emotions in education.* New York, NY: Routledge.

OECD (2017). *PISA 2015 results (volume III): Students' well-being.* Paris: OECD Publishing.

OECD (2019). *PISA 2018 results (volume III): What school life means for students' lives.* Paris: OECD Publishing.

Ramirez, G., Shaw, S. T., & Maloney, E. A. (2018). Math anxiety: Past research, promising interventions, and a new interpretation framework. *Educational Psychologist, 53,* 145–164.

Sarason, I. G., & Sarason, B. R. (1990). *Test anxiety.* In H. Leitenberg (Ed.). *Handbook of social and evaluation anxiety* (pp. 475–495). Boston, MA: Springer.

von der Embse, N., Jester, D., Roy, D., & Post, J. (2018). Test anxiety effects, predictors, and correlates: A 30-year meta-analytic review. *Journal of Affective Disorders, 227,* 483–493.

Zeidner, M. (1995). Adaptive coping with test situations: A review of the literature. *Educational Psychologist, 30,* 123–133.

Zeidner, M. (1998). *Test anxiety: The state of the art.* New York, NY: Plenum.

Zeidner, M. (2014). Anxiety in education. In R. Pekrun, & L. Linnenbrink-Garcia (Eds.). *International handbook of emotions in education* (pp. 265–288). New York, NY: Routledge.

Zeidner, M. (2020). Test anxiety. In B. J. Carducci, C. S. Nave, A. D. Fabio, D. H., Saklofske, & C. Stough (Eds.), *The Wiley encyclopedia of personality and individual differences: Models and theories.* Hoboken, NJ: John Wiley & Sons.

9 BUT I TEACH WELL, DON'T I?

Alice Marshall, a 3rd Grade teacher, was having a bad day! She vented her problems on her soul mate, Bob, also a 3rd Grade teacher. 'The kids are just hopeless today! They came in noisily and took forever to get settled. They are lazy and disruptive, giggling and laughing at everything I do. I've had to shout a million times to get them to just pay some attention. As if I don't have enough to put up with! The photocopier won't work so I didn't have enough work sheets. I've had umpteen dozen interruptions, and I've got a headache! Bloody kids, I wish they were more motivated.'

Even students who appear quite motivated in one classroom or learning setting may appear poorly motivated in another. Some teachers get a good response from particular students, but not from others, while other teachers

DOI: 10.4324/9781003198383-10

never seem to get a positive response from most students even when the students are positively disposed to learning.

HAVE YOU ENCOUNTERED SIMILAR CHALLENGES?

Consider some personal classroom management problems you have had, reflect upon those experiences, and describe and unpack them in the following activity.

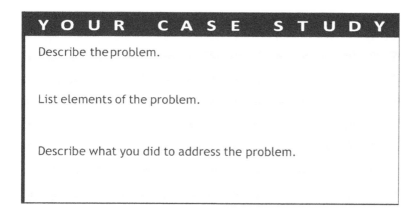

YOUR CASE STUDY

Describe the problem.

List elements of the problem.

Describe what you did to address the problem.

WHAT MIGHT BE THE PROBLEM?

The way teachers perform their teaching role has a significant impact not only on how well students learn, but also on how motivated they are to learn. Teaching was often conceptualized in the past as an active process, while learning was considered relatively passive. In other words, good learning was the result of what the teacher did to students, rather than what the students did. Many of the teaching practices based upon this model inhibited motivation for many children.

Among teaching practices that may inhibit motivation are the following: poor organization; poor discipline and management practices; routinization; authoritarian control; drill and practice routines; learning activities that bear little relationship to student interests and perceived needs; inappropriate difficulty levels (work that is too easy or too hard); unclear expectations in assigned work; unfair marking and grading; undue emphasis on assessment; competitiveness and excessive social comparison among students; lack of resources; students ridiculing each other; poor modelling of attitudes; impersonal, detached, and uncaring teachers; and favoritism.

Good teachers strive to meet students' personal, emotional, and cognitive needs, and when they do so, they enhance student motivation for learning. Effective teachers provide an emotionally safe environment and model risk taking in a safe environment. The classrooms of these teachers are tolerant of mistakes. Learning occurs in a warm interpersonal context in which the development of self-confidence, belonging, personal control, recognition, and autonomy are supported.

Teachers can create meaningful and positive classroom environments by using teaching strategies that meet students' basic affective, learning, and motivational needs. Among the features of classrooms that are important to facilitate this are the following: a physically safe environment; cooperation between teachers and students and an encouragement of mutual respect; attractive, well-resourced, and stimulating learning environments; variety in curriculum and teaching approaches; active involvement in learning; low competitiveness; clear rules and good organization; teaching for learning outcomes; setting appropriate instructional objectives; demonstrating appropriate knowledge; implementing effective questioning techniques; using motivational strategies; monitoring and evaluating student learning; communicating enthusiasm, warmth, and humor; monitoring and evaluating student learning; utilizing appropriate management skills; and a sense of efficacy in both students and teacher.

THINGS TO TRY

In a sense, all of the topics covered in this book give you the wherewithal to redesign your teaching environment to foster motivation and thereby facilitate learning. The following strategies to enhance motivation in your classrooms reflect what we have covered throughout the text (see Table 9.1). Reconsider them now before we look at redesigning the school and classroom contexts to reflect these.

Changing the School's and Classroom's Psychological Environment to Enhance Student Motivation

It is clear that to enhance students' motivation, we must enhance school and classroom practices. This has sometimes been labelled as changing the school's and classroom's 'psychological environment.' There is a need to change a lot of the messages that schools and classrooms communicate to students about the purposes of learning in particular and schooling in general. Key areas include the policies and practices related to rewards, praise, and recognition, the nature of school tasks, grouping and evaluation practices, and resource allocation. A number of these have been covered in earlier sections of the book. Our research and the research of an increasingly large group of educators has shown that the personal engagement of students in learning seems to be most affected by the sense of self that individuals have in the school context. The expectations that individuals hold for themselves as they generalize from

Table 9.1 Essentials of Effective Strategies to Facilitate Motivation

Reducing social comparison by

- avoiding external and public evaluation;
- emphasizing achievement in terms of improvement, progress, and personal best rather than in terms of comparative norms reflected through grades and marks;
- using a range of measurement, evaluation, and reporting schemes; and
- using evaluation that relates to the 'real world' of the student.

Stimulating student involvement in learning by

- using variety in your teaching methods (including group work, peer tutoring, games and simulations);
- allowing students choice and control over their learning-related to method, pace, and content; and
- situating learning in relevant 'real life' contexts.

Focusing on effort by

- emphasizing personal effort as the means for improvement;
- helping students see that mistakes are part of learning;
- setting realistic expectations on 'reasonable effort'; and
- helping students establish realistic goals.

Promoting competence beliefs by

- helping students develop metacognitive and self-regulatory skills;
- communicating positive expectations;
- making plans with students for improvement; and
- assigning optimally challenging tasks.

Increasing chances for success by

- modelling learning approaches and motivation in the classroom;
- teaching learning skills and strategies;
- individualizing instruction; and
- using cooperative and peer learning situations.

past experiences and incorporate the more immediate expectations of parents, teachers, and peers profoundly affect motivation and performance levels. Learners' sense of self, reflected through a sense of competence and of purpose of schooling, and the extent to which they see the relevance of what they learn in school to their lives and future, are critical to their motivation, academic achievement, and retention at school (see, e.g., Oyserman, 2015).

Sense of competence relates to an individual's self-concept for the task of learning: how one assesses one's capacity to learn. A sense of competence is a major determinant of students' school confidence, how much they like school, their level of attendance, and the goals that they set for themselves while at school and later. Our research has shown that students who feel incompetent dislike school, have limited educational and occupational aspirations, as well as have high absenteeism and lower classroom grades.

Students who have a strong and clear sense of self and of purpose of schooling value learning more, intend to complete school, perform better academically at school and desire more prestigious occupations after leaving school than those who do not have a strong and clear sense of self and of purpose of schooling. Clearly, those students who set academic goals and see a purpose in schooling are more likely to be successful in that context. In other words, when students see the importance of schooling and of what they learn in school for their personal growth and life beyond school, they are more motivated than those who do not.

The motivation literature has suggested that level of adaptive motivation, such as striving for excellence in one's work and desiring improvement against personal standards, strongly predicted a student's engagement and commitment to learning. On the other hand, competition and extrinsic rewards were either unimportant or contradictory to the best interests of the students. That is, competition is typically associated with students' fear of failure, sense of pressure, and anxiety. As a result, students are inhibited in giving their best effort and realizing their potential.

Diagnosing Current School Practice

Many schools and classrooms do not implement policies and practices that are in the best interests of motivating students. In some cases, school practices actually run counter to effective motivation strategies within classroom settings. For example, a teacher may work very hard to encourage students' intrinsic interest in reading, only to have the school executive decide to implement a commercial program where rewards and incentives become a goal. Or, a teacher may decide to grade according to improvement, only to have this undermined by a normative assessment program across grades. Teachers may provide recognition on the basis of progress, improvement, and effort, while the school rewards relative ability. Obviously, best instructional and assessment practices must be introduced, socialized, and internalized by teachers before they can be consistently carried out both across classrooms and in the school as a whole.

Borrowing an acronym, TARGET, from Epstein (1989), Martin Maehr and his colleagues (Maehr & Anderman, 1993; Maehr & Midgley, 1991, 1996) developed a framework which may be employed to guide the development of a school-wide emphasis on mastery goals in learning rather than performance goals (refer back to Chapter 7 – *Shooting for Goals*). TARGET is a process for effectively assessing current practices within a school or classroom, as well as future directions in order to integrate and implement the findings, discussed above, on what practices are most likely to facilitate the intrinsic motivation and to foster the mastery orientation of students in learning. The acronym stands for:

* Task
* Authority
* Recognition

- Grouping
- Evaluation
- Time

Within each of the TARGET areas, teachers and administrators can use strategies that either focus on task and social solidarity goals, or on ego and extrinsic goals. Maehr and Midgley (1991, p. 404) make the following points:

> *Teachers can and do define the nature of academic Tasks. Thus, they may make specific attempts to give their students challenging learning experiences. They may attempt to select activities that are interesting and intrinsically engaging. Similarly, teachers make significant decisions regarding how they will share Authority or distribute responsibility; they Reward and Recognize students for different reasons, for improvement, progress, or for comparative performance; they Group children differently and thereby emphasize or de-emphasize interpersonal competition and social comparison; they certainly Evaluate in various ways and on various bases. Finally, teachers choose to use Time allotted to them in certain ways and, of course, significantly control the scheduling of learning. To some degree, all of these factors seem to contribute to an overall sense of what learning in a particular classroom, at least, is about. Such strategies as those grouped in the so-called TARGET categories serve to communicate to students the purpose for learning in a given situation.*

Table 9.2 presents some ideas based on the TARGET principles for you to try to optimize the motivation of your students in your classrooms.

Adolescence and School Motivation – Are There Special Issues?

It is a common experience of teachers that younger students are easier to motivate academically than adolescents. There is clear evidence that there is a decline in school motivation for many students as they move from primary grades to high school. Research tends to support the view that motivation is a serious issue during adolescence, and whether adolescent students are motivated academically may have major consequences for later life choices.

What are the causes of this decline in school motivation? Studies suggest that declines in motivation during adolescence are associated with contextual/environmental factors and are not simply the result of pubertal changes. According to a stage-environment fit model (Eccles, 1993; Eccles & Midgley, 1989; Eccles & Roeser, 2010), there is a direct link between the decline in motivation and changes in classroom learning environments as children move into secondary grades, with a number of researchers suggesting that instructional practices and educational policies of secondary schools may be inappropriate for maintaining student motivation.

Secondary schools, for example, emphasize comparative student performance through exams and assignments much more than primary schools. This perhaps is one reason why, as children grow older, they become more convinced that ability is relatively fixed and that expenditure of effort,

Table 9.2 General Framework Employed in Developing a School-wide Emphasis to Enhance Motivation

TARGET Area	Focus	Goals	Strategies
Task	Valuing and enjoying learning.	To reduce the reliance on extrinsic incentives.	Use programs that take advantage of students' back-grounds and experiences.
			Avoid extrinsic rewards for achievement.
		To design programs that are appropriate, interesting, and challenging.	
		To stress goals and purposes in learning.	Foster programs that stress goal-setting and self-regulation/management.
		To stress the fun of learning.	Implement programs that make use of learning in a variety of non-school settings.
		To give children the opportunity to feel competent.	Individualize tasks to some degree so that all students are not working on the same task.
Authority	Student participation in school/classroom–decisions.	To provide opportunities to develop responsibility, independence, and leadership skills in learning activities.	Give optimal choice in learning activities.
		To develop skills in self-regulation of learning behavior.	Give opportunities to learn metacognitive strategies for self-regulation.
		To develop skills in personal goal setting.	Give opportunities for self-evaluation in learning activities.
Recognition	The nature and use of recognition and reward for learning achievement.	To provide opportunities for all students to be recognized.	Foster 'personal best' awards.
		To recognize progress in goal attainment.	Foster policy in which all students and their learning achievements can be recognized.
		To recognize efforts in a broad array of learning activities.	
Grouping	Student interaction, social skills.	To build an environment of acceptance and appreciation of all students.	Provide opportunities for cooperative learning and values learning, problem solving, and decision making.

(Continued)

Table 9.2 General Framework Employed in Developing a School-wide Emphasis to Enhance Motivation (*Continued*)

TARGET Area	Focus	Goals	Strategies
		To broaden range of social interaction, particularly with at-risk students.	Allow time and opportunity for peer interaction to occur.
		To enhance social skills development.	Foster the development of subgroups (teams, schools within schools, etc.) within which significant interaction can occur.
		To encourage humane values.	Encourage flexible group membership to increase range of peer interaction and to reduce social comparison.
		To build an environment in which all can see themselves as capable of making significant contributions.	
Evaluation	The nature and use of evaluation and assessment procedures in learning activities.	To increase students' sense of competence and self-efficacy.	Reduce emphasis on social comparisons of achievement by minimizing public reference to normative evaluation standards (e.g., grades and test scores).
		To increase students' awareness of progress in developing skills and understanding.	Establish policies and procedures which give students opportunities to improve their performance (e.g., study skills training).
		To increase students' appreciation of their unique set of talents.	Create opportunities for students to assess progress toward goals they have set.
		To increase students' acceptance of failure as a natural part of learning and life.	
Time	The management of time in learning programs.	To improve rate of work completion.	Provide experience in personal goal-setting and in monitoring progress in carrying out plans for goal achievement.
		To improve skills in planning and organizing.	Foster opportunities to develop time-management skills.
		To improve self-management ability.	Allow students to progress at their own rate whenever possible.
		To allow the learning task and student needs to dictate scheduling.	Encourage flexibility in the scheduling of learning experiences.

particularly in an activity in which one is not very successful, demonstrates a lack of competence to others. Consequently, many individuals avoid putting in effort simply to avoid being labelled 'stupid.' Through their assessment and evaluation policies and practices, many secondary schools do not encourage adolescents to become academic 'risk takers.'

Adolescents seek opportunities for developing a sense of self-efficacy and autonomy. We see this commonly demonstrated through the way in which adult power is constantly challenged by adolescents (just ask any parent of an adolescent child!). Secondary schools, by and large, are very regimented places in which the power hierarchy is quite explicit, both within and outside the classroom. With little opportunity to take charge of their own learning and motivation in such a context, many adolescent students simply oppose or withdraw from engagement.

Many primary classrooms emphasize the fun of learning and captivate students more intrinsically in activities, with some school systems even eliminating examination for lower primary levels. Who said that adolescents no longer want or need to be captivated? Yet, many secondary classrooms are crushingly dull places to learn. It is still common to hear of teachers who engage their students in monotonous rote recall activities such as copying notes off the board. With little real stimulation in many classrooms, students will engage in a diverse range of more stimulating, non–academic activities. In this instance, it is not a case of adolescents lacking motivation but, rather, of them investing their motivational energy in the wrong activities for the lack of something better at school. We hope that the strategies that we have outlined and shared with you in this book help you in fostering the motivation, engagement, and well-being of your students. We hope these strategies help your students achieve their best and, in the process, facilitate your own professional growth and personal development as teachers and as individuals.

QUESTION POINTS

?	To what extent have you implemented TARGET-based practices in the classroom? Which principle(s) do you think do you find most effective in motivating classroom learning of your students? Discuss the possible reasons why you think that may be the case.
?	Using the different perspectives of motivation that you have learned in this book, reflect upon your own motivation as a teacher. What motivate you to do well in your teaching profession? How does this motivation impact the ways in which you invest your time and energy to do well in your profession and, in turn, your students' motivation and engagement?

ACTION STATIONS

- Even when students are initially interested in a topic, attention may drop at times. Observe how classroom teachers maintain student attention during a lesson or group work. Techniques might include variability (e.g., the use of aids, group dynamics, and sensory modalities), attention cues (e.g., 'this is very important,' or bells and claps), accountability (e.g., structured cooperative activities involving designated roles), and questioning (a general question to the whole class before individual questions are directed to specific students). There are many others. Remember that the most important element in motivation is the initial interest. Attention-gaining techniques may simply be reduced to razzamatazz unless the learning activity itself is meaningful, relevant, and interesting to the students. So, we would like to encourage you to:
  - ⋆ Observe and discuss with your colleagues the ways in which attention is gained and maintained in the classroom.
  - ⋆ Record your observations.
  - ⋆ Have a colleague complete the same observations on your lessons. Compare your notes.
- Revisit your personal case study and describe your new insights and solutions.

REFERENCES AND RECOMMENDED READINGS

Anderman, E. M. (2021). *Sparking student motivation: The power of teachers in rekindling a love of learning.* Thousand Oaks, CA: Corwin.

Bardach, L., Oczlon, S., Pietschnig, J., & Lüftenegger, M. (2020). Has achievement goal theory been right? A meta-analysis of the relation between goal structures and personal achievement goals. *Journal of Educational Psychology, 112,* 1197–1220.

Eccles, J. S. (1993). School and family effects on the ontogeny of children's interests, self-perceptions, and activity choice. In J. Jacobs (Ed.). *Nebraska Symposium on motivation, 1992: Developmental perspectives on motivation* (pp. 145–208). Lincoln, NE: University of Nebraska Press.

Eccles, J. S., & Midgley, C. (1989). Stage/environment fit: Developmentally appropriate classrooms for early adolescents. In R. Ames, & C. Ames (Eds.), *Research on motivation in education* (Vol. 3, pp. 139–181). New York, NY: Academic Press.

Eccles, J. S., & Roeser, R. W. (2010). An ecological view of schools and development. In J. L. Meece, & J. S. Eccles (Eds.). *Handbook of research on schools, schooling, and human development* (pp. 6–21). New York, NY: Routledge.

Elliot, A. J., & Hulleman, C. S. (2017). Achievement goals. In A. J. Elliot, C. S. Dweck, & D. S. Yeager (Eds.). *Handbook of competence and motivation: Theory and application* (pp. 43–60). New York, NY: The Guilford Press.

Epstein, J. (1989). Family structures and student motivation: A developmental perspective. In C. Ames & R. Ames (Eds.), *Research in motivation in education (Vol. 3): Goals and cognitions.* New York, NY: Academic.

Iaconelli, R., & Anderman, E. A. (2021). Classroom goal structures and communication style: The role of teacher immediacy and relevance-making in students' perceptions of the classroom. *Social Psychology of Education, 24*, 37–58.

Lüftenegger, M., Tran, U. S., Bardach, L., Schober, B., & Spiel, C. (2017). Measuring a mastery goal structure using the TARGET framework: Development and validation of a classroom goal structure questionnaire. *Zeitschrift für Psychologie, 225*, 64–75.

Maehr, M. L., & Anderman, E. M. (1993). Reinventing schools for early adolescents: Emphasizing task goals. *The Elementary School Journal, 93*, 593–610.

Maehr, M. L., & Midgley, C. (1991). Enhancing student motivation: A school-wide approach. *Educational Psychologist, 26*, 399–427.

Maehr, M. L., & Midgley, C. (1996). *Transforming school culture.* Boulder, CO: Westview Press.

Oyserman, D. (2015). *Pathways to success through identity-based motivation.* Oxford: Oxford University Press.

Wentzel, K. R. (2020). *Motivating students to learn* (5th ed.). New York, NY: Routledge.

Wentzel, K. R., & Miele, D. B. (2016). *Handbook of motivation at school* (2nd ed.). New York, NY: Routledge.

Index

Page numbers in **bold** refer to tables.

ABC program *Play School* 15
ability 3, 4, 16, 17, 21–28, 30–38, 41–48, 67–69, 70, 72, 74, 81, 84, 86, 94, 95–96; cross-over effect of 37; fixed mindset of 33; growth mindset of 33; malleability of 33; positive or negative beliefs about 34
achievement 10, 17–18, 22–28, 30, 32–36, 38, 44, 66, 69–71, 73–75, 78, 79–84, 87–88, 93
Achievement Emotion Theory 79, **80**
achiever *see* high-need achiever; low-need achiever
adolescence 95–98
aesthetic needs 13
alleviating test anxiety 84–87
amotivated students 12
anger 35, 79, **80**, 81, 84
anti-intellectual places 24
anxiety 77–88; effective reduction of 85; school motivation and 81–83; sense of 94; severe 81; signs of 87; social 46; state 82; test **69**, 78–79, **80**, 82, 84–87; trait 82
Applied Behavior Analysis 58
attainment value 23
attribution factors 31–39: ability 3, 4, 16, 17, 21–28, 30–38, 41–48, 67–69, 70, 72, 74, 81,84, 86, 94, 95–96; ease of task 34; effective strategies 28, 33, 68, 84, **93**; effort 5, 12–13, 17–18, 24–28, 30, 32–38, 44–48, 51, 55, 64–74, 78, 86, 93–96, 98; luck 31–34, 37; origin 37–38; pawn 37–38
attributional retraining 38
Attribution Theory 31–39; *see also* attribution factors

autonomy-supportive motivating style 12, 17; acknowledgment of, and response to, students' negative affect 13; communication of values and rationale of tasks 13; language use 12; nurturance of motivational resources 12
avoidance-oriented coping 85

Battle Hymn of the Tiger Mother 56
behavioral teaching, programmatic approaches to 58–59
behavioral theories 5
behaviorism 53
belongingness and love needs 13
biological and physiological needs 13
boredom 14, 79, **80**
Broaden-and-Build Theory 83

causes for success and failure of students 32
Cognitive-Behavioral Therapy (CBT) 87
cognitive disequilibrium 14
cognitive needs 13, 92
cognitive theories 5; *see also* Social-Cognitive Theory
computer software programs 15
confidence 41–49
contentment 79, **80**
continuous reinforcement 52
Control-Value Model of Achievement Emotion 81
cooperative learning 18; *see also* peer learning
corporal punishment 56
Corrective Reading 59
curiosity as a need for cognition 13–14, 15
curious students 13–14

deficiency needs 13
Direct Instruction 59–62; as a cognitive
  strategy 60; as a teaching procedure
  59–60
Direct Instruction System in Arithmetic
  and Reading (DISTAR) 59
Direct or Indirect Teaching 60–62
disappointment 32, 79, **80**
disequilibrium *see* cognitive
  disequilibrium

effort 5, 12–13, 17–18, 24–28, 30, 32–38,
  44–48, 51, 55, 64–74, 78, 86, 93–96, 98
emotions 1, 5–6, 32, 35, 78–79, **80**,
  81–85, 88; achievement 10, 17–18,
  22–28, 30, 32–36, 38, 44, 66, 69–71,
  73–75, 78, 79–84, 87–88, 93; anger
  35, 79, **80**, 81, 84; anticipatory **80**,
  85; boredom 14, 79, **80**; contentment
  79, **80**; disappointment 32, 79, **80**;
  enjoyment 11, 23, 79, **80**, 81, 84;
  frustration 13, 32, **80**, 81, 84; gratitude
  79, **80**, 84; hope 1, 6, 66, 79, **80**, 98;
  hopelessness 79, **80**; pride 32, 34, 67,
  79, **80**; promoting regulation of 83–84;
  relaxation 79, **80**, 84, 86–87; relief 79,
  80; RULER 83–84; sadness 79, **80**, 81;
  shame 35, 79, **80**; *see also* anxiety
emotion-focused coping 85
emotion regulatory skills 83–84
enjoyment 11, 23, 79, **80**, 81, 84
essentials of effective strategies to facilitate
  motivation **93**
esteem needs 13
expectancy: of academic success 26;
  beliefs 23; of success and value 23; of
  success or failure 22
Expectancy-Value Theory 22, 23, 26, 27,
  31
Explicit Teaching 60
extrinsic 54
extrinsic motivation 10, 79
extrinsic rewards 73, 94
extrinsic token rewards 55

failure-accepting students 24
failure-avoiding students 24
frustration 13, 32, **80**, 81, 84

goals 64–75; characteristics of 67; helping
  students to set 72–73; mastery 66–67,
  68, 94; morality-based 66; orientations
  66; outcome-focused 65; performance
  66–67, **69**; personal investment in

achieving 73–74; process-focused
  65–66; social 66–67, **70**; social
  solidarity 73–74; types of 65
goal-setting skills 43
grade-oriented students 12
gratitude 79, **80**, 84
growth needs 13

high-need achiever 23–25, 34
hope 1, 6, 66, 79, **80**, 98
hopelessness 79, **80**
humanistic theories 5

interest in learning 16
intrinsic interest 18
intrinsic motivation 10–12, 15–17, 55, 79,
  86, 94
intrinsic value 23

knowledge construction process 14

lack of ability 30–39; *see also* ability
lack of interest 14
learned helpless students 24
learner: deep-seated personal
  characteristics of 11; experience 18
learning: active involvement by students
  in 15; activities 79; behavioral
  approach 52; cooperative and peer 18;
  experience 18; goal-setting skills 43;
  highly motivating techniques in 15;
  information-processing or cognitive
  strategies 43; interest in 16; lack of
  interest in 14; mastery-oriented 67;
  principles 45–46; punishment and
  56–57; self-regulated 47–48; student
  interest in 15; teaching planning 43;
  utilize fantasy 15
learning theory 14; *see also* personal
  constructivism
low-need achievement students 25–26
low-need achiever 23–25, 34
luck 33

mastery goals 66–67, 94
mastery motivation 66
mastery-oriented learning 67
mastery-oriented students 24, **68**
mental processing of success or failure 32
metacognitive awareness 16
metacognitive skills 18, 84
mobile game applications 16
model inhibited motivation 91
morality-based goals 66

Morphographic Spelling 59
motivation 2–7; achievement behaviors of students 24; atheoretical explanations of 3; behavioral theories 5; cognitive theories 5; educational environments 4; effective teaching as a 3; extrinsic 10, 79; genesis and maintenance of 5; humanistic theories 5; impacts on learning 3–4; intrinsic 10–12, 15–17, 55, 79, 86, 94; lack of 3–4; to learn 16; of learners 3; literature 94; mastery 66; model inhibited 91; negative forms of 4; Personal Investment Theory of 73; perspectives on 4–6; problem and issue in 10–14, 22–26, 31–36; psychological and/or physiological forces 4–5; school 95–98; Self-Determination Theory 11; Social-Cognitive Theory 5, 42, 47, 79; of students 3–4; successful learning as a 3; of teacher 3; theoretical explanations of 3; theories of 5; variation in 3
multimedia computer software programs 16

National Institute for Direct Instruction (NIFDI) 59
needs *see specific needs*
negative activating emotions 79
negative deactivating emotions 79
negative emotions 79, **80**; *see also* emotions
negative reinforcement 53–54
negative strategies: used to avoid failure by low-need achievement students 25; used to 'guarantee success' by low-need achievement students 25–26
negative thoughts and feelings 11, 16–17
non-tangible rewards 62

observational learning principles 46
Operant Conditioning model of behavior 52
optimally challenging tasks 27
origins 37–38
outcome-focused goals 65

pawns 37–38
peer group 66, 69, 70
peer learning 18; *see also* cooperative learning
peer models 24, 46–47
performance goals 66, 67
performance-oriented students **69**

personal constructivism 14
Personal Investment in achieving goals 73–74
Personal Investment Theory 73
physiologically activating emotions 79
physiologically deactivating emotions 79
positive emotions 37, 79, **80**, 81, 83; *see also* emotions
positive reinforcement 53–54, 57
Positive Teaching 58
Precision Teaching 59
pride 32, 34, 67, 79, **80**
problem-focused coping 85
process-focused goals 65–66
programmatic approaches to behavioral teaching 58–59
psychological environment of classroom 92
punishment 54; appropriate forms of 57–58; communication of anger and 35; corporal 56; defined 56; for incorrect behavior 56; lack of 35; learning and 56–57; motivates behavior through 5; negative reinforcement as 53; response cost 57; reward and 56; sympathetic and withholding 36; unpleasant association 54

reinforcement: continuous 52; negative 53–54; positive 53–54, 57; problems with 54–56; self-reinforcement 47; stars, stamps, and jelly beans 51–62
relaxation 79, **80**, 84, 86–87
relief 79, **80**
response cost 57
reward 55; anticipated 23; application of 52; appropriate 27; on basis of good performance 47; extrinsic 59, 73, 94; extrinsic token 55; human motivation 55; lack of 17; motivates behavior through 5; non-tangible 62; pleasant 53; positive reinforcement 53; predetermined goal through 59; punishment and 56; type of 43; verbal 55
risk-taking behavior 27
RULER 83–84

sadnesss 79, **80**, 81
safety needs 13
school motivation 95–98
school's and classroom's psychological environment 92–94

school-wide emphasis to enhance motivation **96–97**
secondary schools 95–96
self-actualization needs 13
self-agentic 48
self-concept 4, 93
self-confidence 45
self-determination 43
Self-Determination Theory 11–13; extrinsically motivated students 11–12; intrinsically motivated students 11; need for autonomy 11; need for competence 11; need for relatedness 11; psychological needs 11
self-efficacy 18, 38, 42–45, 48, 85; modeling 45–46; peer models and 46–47; self-regulation and 46; sense of 98; sources of 43
self-esteem 27, 35–37, 82
self-handicapping strategies 25
self-management 47–48
self-regulated learning 47–48
self-regulated students 48
self-regulatory skills 18
self-reinforcement 47
self-sabotaging behaviors 4
self-sabotaging strategies 25
self-worth-focused students 24
Self-Worth Theory 24
severe anxiety 81
shame 35, 79, **80**
situational interest 15–16
social anxiety 46
Social-Cognitive Theory 5, 42, 47, 79
social comparison 18, 27, 42, 55, 69, 71–72, 74, 81, 91, 93, 95, 97
social goals 66, 69–70
socially-oriented students **70**
social solidarity goals 73–74
stage-environment fit model 95
state anxiety 82
students: achievement behaviors of 24; amotivated 12; causes for success and failure 32–33; complex history of 1; curious 13–14; extrinsically motivated 11–12; failure-accepting 24; failure-avoiding 24; grade-oriented 12; highly motivated 3; interest in learning 15;

intrinsically motivated 11, 13; intrinsic motivation 16; involvement in learning activities 15; learned helpless 24; mastery-oriented 24, **68**; natural motivation 16; needs for competence, autonomy, and relatedness of 11, 15; negative thoughts and feelings 11, 16–17; performance-oriented **69**; personal effort 18; reasonable effort 18; self-efficacy 43; self-regulated 48; self-worth-focused 24; socially-oriented **70**; socioeconomic and family backgrounds 3; task-focused 24; varies in motivation 3; *see also see* motivation
success or failure: expectancy of 22; mental processing of 32; in terms of rewards 23

tall intellectual poppies 24
TARGET 94–95
task difficulty 33
task-focused students 24
task-irrelevant thoughts 82
teachers: autonomy-supportive 12; cognitive disequilibrium by 14; familiar with classes and individuals 3; feedback of 34; knowledge construction process 14; motivation of 3
teaching planning 43
teaching strategies 92
television programs 19; *ABC Play School* 15; *Sesame Street* 19; *The Simpsons* 19
test anxiety **69**, 78–79, **80**, 82, 84–87
theoretical personality types 23; *see also* high-need achiever; low-need achiever
Time out 59
trait anxiety 82
transcendence needs 13

unmotivated learning behavior 50–62
utility value 23

value *see* specific value
verbal rebuke 57
verbal rewards 55

Yale Center of Emotional Intelligence 83

For Product Safety Concerns and Information please contact our EU
representative GPSR@taylorandfrancis.com
Taylor & Francis Verlag GmbH, Kaufingerstraße 24, 80331 München, Germany

www.ingramcontent.com/pod-product-compliance
Ingram Content Group UK Ltd.
Pitfield, Milton Keynes, MK11 3LW, UK
UKHW021456080625
459435UK00012B/525